Accidental Anthropologists

A Memoir

Claudia Clavel

Published by: Pajarito Graphics
Email: pajaritographics@gmail.com

ISBN-13: 978-1502557711

ISBN-10: **1502557711**

Dec. 2014

For Joan
I hope you enjoy
my book

Claudia Claudel
aka
Julie's Mom

DEDICATION

This book is dedicated to the Perfectos and Pilars of Northern New Mexico. It is their ancestral Spanish spirituality, practical wisdom and humor that continue to hold their culture together. Thomas and I feel fortunate that we stumbled into their world. Being a part of it has opened an entirely new view of life to our family. Because of it, we have grown more tolerant, patient and sensitive to everything around us.

Viva la gente!

Contents

Introduction

When we returned to Northern New Mexico thirty years ago, I was struck by the listing of names in our little rural phone book; they were positively lyrical. There were names like: Soledad, Eusebio, Filedelfia, Estefanita, Filemon, Eloyda, Zoila; page after page of beautifully descriptive names of up to five syllables, thoughtfully given to newborns. I have been fortunate during those years to know some of the people baptized with these archaic Spanish names, and it makes me wonder whether there are people living in Spain today who are still being addressed by equally poetic nouns. For years, I have been reading obituaries just so I can enjoy rolling such romantic sounds off my tongue.

It was only recently, as I scanned the obituary columns, that I noticed the vast difference between ages and names within a family. Most often, if the deceased was quite elderly, not only are the grandchildren's names listed but also those of great-grandchildren. It was that discovery that led me to the awareness of the old-fashioned Hispanic names that are slipping away in the face of modernity. In fact, it came as a huge shock, as I was reading through the obits a few days ago, to learn that within three to four generations, the beautiful old sounds had disappeared completely.

For example, there is Tranquelino, age 94, and his brothers: Primitivo, Requier, Elizardo, Venancio, Baltazar and Teofilo; his sisters: Eufelia, Guadalupita, Trementina, Christalina and Maclovia, followed by his sons: Robert, Paul, Joseph, John and Peter. Continuing with his daughters: Teresa, Mary, Anna and Christine, followed by his grandsons, Frank, Randy, Matthew, and granddaughters, Angela, Melissa and Mikelah. In addition, at the end of the list, Tranquilino's great-grandsons with very modern names of one and two syllables: Tyler, Jordan, and Cory; and great-granddaughters, Venus, April and Dawn.

Over the years, I have watched my elderly neighbors pass through their lives while babies are being born to replace them, but without those beautiful old names being passed on. I have watched those children grow into adulthood, marry and inhabit the homes of their grandparents. Even though they still keep the tradition of cutting and heating with wood, the old-fashioned names have become as ethereal as the smoke that rises from their chimneys. In many ways, I think the culture is just as strong as ever, for there are some things that never change; habits and traditions that are woven into the fabric of their lives. But how I long for some of those beautiful old names to be carried on, so I can continue rolling them over and over on my tongue.

In order to protect the privacy of my neighbors I have chosen to change the names of real people in my stories using some of those old classic names. It has given me much pleasure to choose names, which reflect a number of personalities as much as possible.

The names of people with no direct connection to the area are real, including movie personnel.

Because of the reserved nature among the people of the area I wanted to be sure my stories would not offend anyone, especially in the case of illness, because thirty years ago that topic was not discussed outside the home. That led me directly to Pilar and Perfecto, because I had written about Pilar's illness in their story. It was important because her brain aneurism was pivotal to our friendship. I read their story to them one blustery winter afternoon and asked for comments and criticism when I finished. I had to smile when Pilar said, "Claudia, you described me perfectly." Perfecto added, "That's her alright." I asked whether they thought I had exaggerated any of the details, and they assured me I had not. We agreed that Pilar was a heroic figure under the circumstance and her story was worth telling. She had become an inspiration to others in the area.

It took months for me to gather enough courage to approach my neighbors again and read all of the less than humorous stories. I simply could not publish this book without their approval, and it had been keeping me up at night. The three of us sat at their kitchen table on a late summer afternoon, and I read for nearly three hours. Pilar and Perfecto were thoughtful listeners and urged me to continue reading, story after story.

When I finished, we all sat quietly for a while and finally I asked, "Well, can you deal with this? Have I gone too far?" Perfecto began to speak softly as he said, "You know, I wouldn't like these stories if you had made them up. But because they are true, and real, I really like them. They tell who we are. And how we live our lives here. I tell the same kind of stories when our family gathers. I want my children and grandchildren to know this is the way life is here. It's part of our culture. You have written about a thirty year slice of history in San Ignacio."

I looked at Pilar, and she added, "I could listen to your stories all day. This was better than watching a *telanovela*."

1

Big Truck Takes a Trip

It took five months, or nearly two seasons to get our worldly possessions from northern California to northern New Mexico. We bought a 1962 Ford cattle truck from a rancher who swore it would make a fine moving van for us. We were probably too thrifty in thinking the two thousand dollar investment made more sense than the cost of a moving company.

My husband, Thomas lined the high rack sides with plywood. The truck deck had been replaced with redwood planks, sturdy enough for two rusted wood cook stoves that we bought on the cheap from a hoarder. The stoves had been outdoors for years in a place where there was more rain than sun. From the beginning, we gave the battered old truck a title: Big Truck. It had suffered the same fate as the stoves, and the hood was covered with moss and rust. Every time a door slammed, a cloud of rust puffed into the air. However, none of that deterred us. When the ugly beast was filled with our prized possessions, Thomas covered the top with more plywood and we were ready to roll.

We set off in heavy rain in mid-November 1983. I would be following Big Truck in our little yellow Honda, with a small table tied on the roof, its legs reaching skyward like antennae. We had no way of communicating except by intuition. Thomas and I, along with the vehicles, were middle aged and a bit worn around the edges. Taken all together, as a group we were a rather comical sight. But we were excited and determined to begin our new creative life as artists in the Land of Enchantment. Sadly, we didn't get very far.

After about a half hour Big Truck made it twenty-five miles, and then the entire windshield wiper motor and blades fell through the rusted hood. It was dark, and in the pouring rain Thomas could barely see anything. Thankfully we had reached our friends, Chuck and Sally, who lived on a farm right on the highway, so we pulled in and were received with great excitement. Three youngsters, Kendra, Matt and Lindsay, were dancing around the kitchen, caught up in our adventure. The whole family thought of us as a Robinson Crusoe tale about to unfold. I asked if they would fix us a drink.

Chuck directed Thomas and Big Truck into his mammoth barn, while Sally and I prepared the evening meal. During dinner we discussed what we should do next. After checking the weather in New Mexico and seeing stormy weather ahead, we decided to leave the truck in the Dwelley barn and head off in the little yellow Honda the next day. It would be some time before we returned to make repairs and start once again. Our friends assured us it wasn't an inconvenience to leave Big Truck there. Their barn was so big, the truck looked like a toy.

We had rented a mission house from the Presbyterian Church in a very remote New Mexico valley in the Sangre de Cristo Mountains. For more than a couple hundred years Alta Vista had been inhabited by people with beautiful old, Spanish names, who spoke an archaic dialect of Castilian, so rare it was unknown outside the area. Every sentence sounded like a question, with a lilting lift at the end. Through mutual friends, Thomas and I met in Alta Vista ten years earlier. We had other friends there, so it wasn't an unfamiliar world to us. That's where we had been headed, in time for winter. Locals called their eighty-five-hundred-foot-high valley Little Alaska. We knew it would be a challenging experience.

In March, working our way through snow showers, Thomas and I returned to California and our friends. Chuck helped get the windshield unit stabilized and we checked in with our CPA, who was doing our taxes. The three of us agreed that he should mail the forms to us in New Mexico in time for the tax deadline. From the Dwelley barn, we set out again on March 27, 1984. The trip would take six weeks, right up to the April 15 deadline, but we didn't know that, so we remained undaunted by what lay ahead.

We hadn't driven a hundred miles when we were pulled over at a temporary vehicle inspection site. The inspector waved us over and then couldn't stop laughing as he walked around kicking tires, bending down to look beneath the frame. A little gasp broke his laughter when he noticed moss growing all over the hood. I prayed he wouldn't open a door because of the rust that would shower down on him. He asked where we were headed and Thomas replied, "New Mexico." The guy laughed again as he said, "Well, I don't want to keep you. I hope you make it."

We made it as far as the San Rafael Bridge at 4:45 p.m. that day, when Big Truck stopped dead in its tracks in a left-turn lane onto the bridge. Traffic was tied up for nearly an hour until Thomas got it started and we lurched ahead. It died again in San Leandro and yet again in Modesto, that time in the middle of an intersection.

Claudia Clavel

Thomas used the starter to goose the ugly beast off the highway. We left it by the side of the road and checked into a motel. By then, we hoped someone would take Big Truck. However, no one did. (And there were plenty of opportunities yet to come.)

The dishonest rancher who sold us the truck became the target of our wrath. We were gutsy but not stupid, we had bought on his word. Still, we weren't ready to give up.

On our final approach to Fresno that second day, we called ahead to my brother, who owned a Ford agency. We needed a mechanic. The entire staff of Fresno Ford lined up to stare in disbelief as Big Truck pulled in and Thomas, the smallish, middle-aged man who piloted the huge rusted relic hopped down from his perch. Manuel, the mechanic, looked up at my brother and said, "No way, man." My towering brother laughed until tears ran down his cheeks. Thomas turned to the mechanic and said, "I think only a Manuel is capable of repairing this thing." We had lived in Mexico for three years and witnessed that kind of genius.

That night, as I sank down in sofa softness, my body felt relieved of a huge responsibility. Following that lumbering beast hour after hour, waiting for anything and everything to happen, had taken a toll. At breakfast, I told of an incident the day before on U.S. 99, when I was behind Thomas and there was a sudden minor explosion ahead, jolting me to full attention. A large ball of fire hit the road beneath the belly of the truck. Big Truck actually rose off the road from the force, and I nearly died of shock. I became a little hysterical by the end of my tale, but took that as a form of relief.

Manuel reluctantly agreed to take on the awesome task of rebuilding the truck's engine. To spare my brother

Accidental Anthropologists

any further embarrassment, we returned to Santa Cruz, where we spent a week and a half with our daughter, Julie. Finally, we were summoned back to Fresno, where Manuel had worked his magic. Then, we set off again. However, we didn't get very far. Seventy-five miles down U.S. 99, a push rod came loose, and we had to return to Fresno Ford for an adjustment. Once again, Chuck's staff waved us off, with cries of, "Good luck! We hope you make it!" You could see pity in their eyes, but once again, we were upbeat and excited to make it over the Sierras.

It was quite an experience, creeping over Tehachapi Pass at twenty-five miles an hour, without benefit of radio or tape deck. At that speed, we had become a road hazard. It was a very quiet trip for us both, and we did a lot of thinking on that stretch.

Finally, just as it was growing dark, the lights of Mojave twinkled up at us. We had made it over the pass, and I was euphoric. There was a near full moon and we felt almost romantic, but then the Big Truck's generator died on the spot. For me, it was the first in a series of highway soft shoulders to cry on. Amazingly, we were across the double divided highway from a Motel 6. We had a bottle of tequila, and by then were pretty certain that Big Truck was too ugly to molest. My spouse and I slept like babes. We had, by God, crossed the Sierras.

We awoke early and headed into Mojave in the little Honda for breakfast and a new generator. It was then I began to notice how many "Soft Shoulder" signs there were along the highway. That meant we were in the desert, and you could get stuck in the soft earth if you pulled off too far. It took five hours in the parking lot of an abandoned gas station with plugged toilets, on the outskirts of town, to right the latest wrong. I was glad not to be a pregnant pioneer, and when I mentioned it to

Thomas, he slid out from beneath the truck to say, "Yeah, if this beast were an ox we'd have to shoot it."

Two hours later, at a roadside rest stop, the truck radiator sprang a leak. Water was streaming through a ruptured seam. Thomas experimented with manifold tube patch and a piece of beer can, and the radiator held for a while. We had attracted a crowd of curious onlookers, who were smiling and shaking their heads as they wished us well. It was growing dark, and a warm breeze lulled us for a few moments as we made the decision to drive until Big Truck stopped of its own accord. Driving at night was better. I couldn't really see the truck in the dark. I could see the tail and brake lights, but by the light of dawn, only the taillights were visible. The brake lights had gone out. And it was then I noticed that the back license plate was gone. My stomach sucked into a knot, because we still had to deal with Arizona Port of Entry. We had been told they were no-nonsense people.

From the seat of my little yellow Honda, surrounded by a pack of gigantic semi trucks and trailers, I thought about Alice in Wonderland and her shrinking pill. Our trip was beginning to feel a bit like that children's story, with all sorts of unexpected events popping up along the way. Finally, we were "called off" with a bunch of other drivers, and Thomas joined the hike to headquarters, papers in hand, knees trembling. That was a tense moment for us both. A while later my spouse emerged, a big grin just breaking. "Let's get the hell out of here before he changes his mind," he laughed. We were doing it! Bit by bit, hour by hour. We had stopped thinking in terms of distance. We were in Arizona. The creative drive was like a tailwind that kept pushing us forward.

The moon was getting bigger, and we got to feeling frisky as the hours rolled by, trouble-free for a change. In

Accidental Anthropologists

Gallup, we stopped for treats and coffee at four in the morning. On we rolled, cruising between fifty and fifty-five miles per hour, mile after mile, up until the next explosion. This blast wasn't as loud as the first one, but it was more dramatic. There was a lot of black smoke, and I watched in horror, as a tire tread emerged through the haze. It was an inside dual tire. There were six tires holding the truck up and the inside tires more difficult to change.

We brushed our teeth, did a few toe touches, took a little walk, and then drove carefully on the next soft shoulder. We weren't far from a motel-café complex and pulled in for breakfast. I walked right to a table of three men. "Any of you know about trucks?" I queried. All three nodded. "How about tires?" I furthered. "We're a road service," a young man answered. Thomas was impressed by my boldness.

We all finished our breakfasts and met out front. The men led us to their place in Navajo, Arizona, which was where they lived and worked. It took five hours instead of twenty minutes. The crew was new at the game, but they were reasonable. They were also very nice people. Thomas and I rested in the shade, read the paper, went for a couple leisurely walks and listened to an array of songbirds in concert to spring. Fifty bucks and a new-used inside dual, and we were rolling toward Albuquerque. It was Sunday, April 15. There were a few hundred miles left to go. No brake lights, no license plate, and we were out of manifold patch. Not only had we left bits and pieces of our former selves behind, in the guise of sold household articles, but we had also scattered remnants of our current selves across the Southwest, including a constant rain of rust. However, we were still feeling hopeful.

Claudia Clavel

As we approached Santa Fe, a huge, squashed, butter-yellow full moon slipped up over a mesa, and we nearly wept in our separate vehicles. Thomas and I drove to the edge of town and a motel. We knew we were close enough to our mountain home to make a run for the mail, no matter what. We felt safe now. Once again, we sipped our tequila and slept like children.

We were up at dawn. A gorgeous day lay ahead. *Huevos rancheros* and strong coffee launched us on our final leg. We felt ecstatic. It had been winter when we left for California six weeks earlier. Now there was spring in the air. You could feel it and see it in the light. We passed our friends' turn-off. I felt a surge of warmth. A mile and a half later, Thomas pulled off to a roadside rest area. A crucial bolt had fallen out of the manifold exhaust system. We were stuck. There were no spare bolts. Rather than chance our friends back down the road, we locked the lumbering giant and set out for home in the little Honda. We raced seventy miles to the tiny post office and were presented with a large box of mail.

At our new home, Thomas and I sat on the front porch, poring over the mail in search of the tax packet. It was there, and we frantically ripped it open. We would get a refund, so no need to worry about a late fine. Our sighs of relief were audible, as we sank down into the warmth of the sun-drenched cement porch, unable to move for a while. Thomas was the one to finally unlock the door and enter the stark adobe house.

It took us a moment to realize that we had been burglarized. After the shock wore off a bit, we took a closer look and saw they had filched a really ugly red rug and two mattresses that belonged to the church. Fortunately, we had previously packed nearly all our things and stored them in the locked attic. Locals probably thought we had

Accidental Anthropologists

burned out on the Alta Vista winter and hie-tailed it back to sunny California. It was that kind of place.

The two of us went back outdoors to sit in the sun and let it all sink in. We were road buzzed and couldn't bear to speak. Eventually, one of us stirred. Our eyes met and held for a long moment. I could feel tears welling up, but then we both started to laugh at the absurdity of it all. We laughed so hard we had to help one another in through the front door. Absence of the ugly red rug sent us into more gales of laughter. We needed food, and one last burst of energy to go fetch Big Truck, hopefully for the last time.

2

Pointed in the Right Direction

It would be more than a year later when Thomas fired up
Big Truck again for our final fateful move. We had started
another silkscreen business as soon as we settled into Alta
Vista and were soon driving hundreds of miles, picking
up and delivering jobs. That was too many miles, and we
knew we had to find another place closer to our clients. As
in most cases regarding our life, the perfect person turned
up at just the right time and pointed us in the right direction. Martina Gomez had been a client for a while, but I
had never met her. Every time Thomas delivered a load of
tee shirts, Martina tried to talk him into looking at her
friend's little adobe house in the village of San Ignacio, a
few miles from her. I was the one who balked at a move,
because I was busy putting my own creative business
venture together. I had created a line of hand-painted
clothing and had just started getting orders from a few
stores in Taos and Santa Fe.

Finally, one day, when Thomas had a load of shirts
for Martina, I joined him for the drive. The woman invited us in for a cup of tea, and it didn't take long for her to
bring up her friend's house. She couldn't stop talking
about it. However, we did learn that Martina was a
vibrant single mom of five children and a community

activist. We took to one another right away. When our tea was finished, Martina threw a jacket over her shoulders and nearly shouted, "This is it, you're going to follow me to the San Ignacio house that I think you should buy. And it's not even out of your way. Claudia, now that I've met you I'm convinced, Mark's little adobe is perfect for you and Thomas."

We followed Martina three or four miles and turned off on a dirt road leading into the village. We drove around the massive, two-hundred-fifty-year-old adobe church in the center of the plaza, kicking up a trail of red dust, and then took a fork in the road leading up to the cemetery. Rows of adobe houses, some in near ruin, lined the four plaza sides. A few little dirt side roads led to other old mud homes on the backside of the village. A sharp right turn took us up to the top of a little narrow mesa, and there at the end, overlooking the village, sat the little adobe house that looked like a bit of a ruin. There was erosion on the south wall and even more on the west side.

The walls were of exposed adobe nearly three feet thick, and you could see little bits of straw and sticks embedded in the petrified mud. The dark brown roof was of rusted corrugated steel with a few edges curled up, and there was a chamber pot full of bullet holes, turned upside-down to cover an old, unused chimney pipe. Next to the house, on the edge of a steep slope to the west, there sat an actual adobe ruin. Martina told us the building had been used for butchering animals and storing canned foods. Thomas got excited over the possibility of restoration. The view from that spot was spectacular.

A huge mesa rose up behind the house to the west, towering over the valley. The land below graduated downward in a series of little mesas, until they finally reached a network of arroyos that all led to the Pecos River.

Accidental Anthropologists

The river ran along two sides of the village, heading south toward the Rio Grande and Mexico. Martina said there were a couple of great swimming holes, and that piqued our interest. By the time we stepped inside the little adobe, I could feel excitement beginning to build between my spouse and me. The shock of the interior sent us into gales of laughter and shouts of "Oh my God!" Martina's friend, Mark had transformed the little three-room adobe into a mini-condo, *à la* Santa Fe.

The builder had taken space out of two rooms in order to create a large bathroom, complete with a sunken tub. On the other side of the wall, Mark had made a little laundry room. The kitchen was huge. There were no interior doors, and he had cut openings in the walls between each room in order to create an open feeling. A *portal*, a long covered cement porch, ran along the east side of the house, and a door in each of the three rooms opened onto it. The living room door was glass, with a bird's eye view of the village stretching out below.

Martina wasn't sure how long the house had been sitting in ruins before her friend bought it. It must have been many years, because we found a lot of initials with dates, from the late 70's and early 80's carved into door-frames. There was a whole history of who had fallen in love with whom over the years. We figured there were probably a number of children who had been conceived within the walls of the old ruin. Between that romantic notion and the sunken bathtub, views, river and picturesque village, we nearly shouted, "We'll take it!" Martina whooped, "I knew it was your place!"

What the woman neglected to mention was the ferocious wind that roared endlessly down from the mountains. And the fact, that at the time, San Ignacio was considered a very dangerous place.

Claudia Clavel

Circa 1985, San Ignacio had one of the most notorious reputations for miles around. The village of around one hundred people held that distinction for many years, and some of the inhabitants were proud of their place in local folklore. When some old friends who lived in a nearby village heard we had bought the place, they begged us to get our money back and get the hell out, pronto. However, after what we had just been through with the move from California, Thomas and I thought we could deal with just about anything. What impressed us most of all was the feeling of raw materials being close at hand for our own creative use. For that was our dream: to create, as much as humanly possible, our own living space. Besides, at $25,000 the price was right.

On moving day Thomas drove the same huge, ugly, lumbering cattle truck seventy miles and two thousand feet lower in elevation to our new home in the timeless New Mexico Spanish village. I was behind him in the little yellow Honda, packed to the roof with overflow. I don't think anyone noticed our grand entrance, except maybe Sixto, who, we were to learn, never missed anything.

The first night we slept in our new home became a test of nerves. The previous owner had covered the outside of all the windows with heavy plastic to help keep out the cold. We hadn't noticed the loose edges, so we were not prepared for the new night sounds. The wind had begun to blow as we were preparing for sleep. Big Truck had not been unloaded, so we slept on the living room floor, beneath the window, in our sleeping bags.

Once the lights were turned off, the excitement began: we could hear mice scurrying around, so we started to sing, thinking that would keep them away. Then the plastic began flapping, louder and louder. The wind grew

Accidental Anthropologists

stronger, and it was then we noticed a new sound: a television antenna on the roof began to rotate in the wind, and with each turn, there was a loud moaning sound. Then the wind began to howl, and the plastic made a whip cracking sound.

It was like being in a house of horrors, and I was suddenly gripped by fear—for what we had chosen for our new life. However, as usual, Thomas started to laugh, and we wound up laughing ourselves to sleep.

3

Settling In

A major problem for us was the fact that we had moved from a twelve-room flat in California. We had too much stuff. Big Truck was almost as big as the three-room adobe. Even though we had sold most of our furniture, the truck's contents would fill the house to the ceiling. There was nothing to do but put most of it in the attic, on top of six inches of ancient earth that served as insulation.

It would take several years before my cartons of art supplies found their way into a donated house that we turned into a studio for me. It took more time than we could have imagined starting a livelihood from scratch, in the middle of nowhere. In addition, as Thomas pointed out many times, "It was always a decision, whether to chop wood to keep us warm, or continue silk-screening in order to feed us." We learned to do both, and that didn't change for several years.

The house had no propane, so everything had to be fueled by wood. One of the last things to be moved in was the better of the two wood cook stoves that we brought from CA. The ugly one would eventually be traded for a big, hand-made pottery table lamp, when an Anglo potter, who specialized in southwest primitive pottery, moved into the village. Mark hadn't finished the bathroom, so there was no lavatory for a while, but we did have the sunken bathtub, and a Miró-esque woven hanging that hung on the back wall over the tub. We also brought a lot of art: paintings and pottery traded with friends or bought on the cheap from struggling artists. Our place was primitive but very artistic. It was enough so to sustain any serious artist through rough times.

Once we had Big Truck unloaded, Thomas got busy turning the slaughterhouse ruin into a workshop for our silkscreen business. The place was a wreck. One end was open, with a *viga*, or roof log, sticking into space. There were only two adobe walls, each standing on top of pieces of flagstone lying on top of the ground. The west wall consisted entirely of linoleum pieces, rusted tin roofing, plywood and even cardboard, crisscrossed with pieces of boards to hold it all in place.

Our friend Florentino Romero came to help Thomas build a new wall. His wife, Lita, and I roasted a turkey while the men worked. Florentino brought three car jacks. They used those to jack the roof up while they tore out all the old materials. The two men framed the wall and then dropped the roof back on. Lita and I heard a huge bang, and I ran out to make sure our men hadn't been killed. Lita said, "Claudia, you don't ever run out to check when men are working. They love all that clanging and banging."

Thomas kept Big Truck around for a year or so, long enough to make a few runs up to the mesa with a neighbor to cut and gather firewood. Moreover, it wouldn't be long before the truck hauled a gift house to our place. We also used Big Truck as a guest room when our friends came from California for a visit that first summer. They asked to sleep in Big Truck in order to experience the incredible night sky. We padded the wood deck, and they climbed into their sleeping bags. Sometime near dawn, a pack of coyotes gathered nearby and began to howl. Bev and Hal swore the pack was on its way up the cattle ramp to devour them in their beds.

It wasn't long before Thomas had his shop up and running, in spite of all its shortcomings. There was a pack rat that dragged rulers, pencils, and, once, a little wrench across the floor in front of Thomas's eyes. Every now and then, he would have to take up the floorboards to retrieve his belongings. Eventually the problem was solved when Thomas scrubbed the pack rat's nest with bleach. More than once, a rabbit hopped into the shop to watch us work, and a bat flew in every evening at dusk.

Thomas and I shared the space for a while until he had a new Santa Fe client who had up to 600 southwest designer tee shirts printed every week. We made a quick trip to Phoenix, where we bought a massive, computerized conveyor-belt dryer and a new six-color printer so that Thomas could keep up with the orders. At one point, we hired a couple of locals to help with silk-screening. One of them worked the evening shift, so the old shop was humming at all hours. I became the pick-up and delivery employee, which was just as well, because I had been forced out of my little creative corner in the shop. The new equipment took up every square inch of space.

Thomas named our business Pajarito Graphics, after a mountain peak above the Chula Vista valley. It wasn't a new name, as he had chosen it thirteen years earlier for a photography business he and a young friend, had started in the valley. It was a nostalgic choice, because this young, gifted photographer took his own life at age 24. Thomas wanted to memorialize their friendship and the wild ride they had for a few months as official school sports photographers in Chula Vista and Santa Teresa.

Claudia Clavel

For about seven years, until Thomas took a job in town, he printed tee shirts and posters for virtually every event from Taos to Santa Fe. It was a great way to meet people and establish relationships that tied us to the community forever. As word spread about Thomas's printing skills, neighbors began turning up on our doorstep with shirt requests for family reunions, community sports events, school projects and fiestas. I was asked to draw many tee shirt designs for religious events, so we met more people up and down the valley.

In the old days, most northern New Mexico villages had at least one *santera* or *santero*: an artist who specialized in religious art. Since daily life revolved around the church, most art was of a religious nature. In our first year in the village, on a lovely fall morning, three neighbors paid me a visit. Catarino, Apolina and Delfinia came to ask if I would help with the San Ignacio float for the San Xavier Fiesta parade. That would be a first for me.

They specifically wanted to feature San Ignacio in some way, and Catarino suggested having the saint's image painted on two 4-by-8-foot sheets of plywood. He wanted to put the paintings on the back of his pickup truck, with an image on each side, facing the spectators along the parade route. The group asked if I would be willing to do the painting.

It was a challenge for me, especially as we had no place for me to work. Catarino said I could paint in the unfinished adobe house he had been working on for a long time. He hadn't put the roof on, so there was plenty of light, and I would be out of the wind. I had recently finished painting a three-fold standing screen with life-size hollyhocks and enjoyed the process immensely. I eagerly agreed to take on the task.

Accidental Anthropologists

Once I had drawn the life-size images of the saints, it occurred to me how much painting had to be done in a short period. I went to see Apolina and Arcenio Tafoya, who were *mayordomos* at the time, and asked for their help in recruiting village teenagers to assist me. I also asked to use their front *portal* for the painting, because Catarino's dirt floors kicked up too much dust as I moved around. I could just imagine the amount of dust with a bunch of teens shuffling around. Besides, the Tafoya *portal* faced north, so the light was perfect. I mixed the paints, and with my little army, we had the job done in two days. The paintings were returned to the adobe house until the fiesta.

On the morning of the parade, a group of us met at Catarino's to load the plywood paintings onto his truck. As we all walked into his house together, we were stopped in our tracks: A ray of early sunlight, coming in through the open roof at an angle, was beamed directly on the painted saints' images. They were positively glowing. There was a collective "Ahh!" and we didn't move for a moment. Apolina broke the silence: "It feels good to have a *santera* in San Ignacio again, after such a long time." To me, it felt like a nice role to have in the village.

One of our first major clients was a man who had been born in the valley but lived in Santa Teresa. Donacio Tafoya was so terrified of San Ignacio that he drove his load of garments to be printed but wouldn't leave them. He was afraid someone, might steal his inventory if he wasn't present. The man sat with me in our kitchen to drink coffee and chat while Thomas printed his shirts and hats. On one trip, Donacio brought us a new picnic table and two benches, so we could sit outdoors in the sun during his wait. He told us his gift was actually a tip, because he thought we were so brave to live in San Ignacio. Another client from the area was running for governor.

Claudia Clavel

Benefacio Zamora also chose to sit at our kitchen table and talk politics with me, while he waited for his posters and shirts to be printed.

To us, our days were filled with endless possibilities. We were constantly stimulated by a parade of interesting people. It felt like everyone genuinely cared about us, and what we were attempting to do, with our business and our life. Over time, Thomas and I cultivated a reputation for being excellent craftspeople and either really brave or completely out of our minds. We agreed that we were a bit of both.

4

The Adventure Begins

Once we became more organized, we were able to explore our new world, and that's when the real adventure began. For the first few months, people had driven to our place, pretending to be lost, in order to check us out. They always ended by asking how we liked living in San Ignacio. We had heard from several neighbors that our place had always been considered a healing spot. For many years, village folks had walked up the hill to sit in the shade of the north wall and soak up healing energy.

I suppose, because of that reputation, I had a couple of interesting visits. The first occurred when a car full of women drove up, honked and waited for me to greet them. Rosina, the driver, said, "Hi Claudia, how are you?" Then she stuck her arm out the window and said rather abruptly, "I have this thing on my arm. What is it?"

That completely threw me, and I stepped back to look at her to see if she was joking. I could see she wasn't and then recognized what I thought her problem might be.

I asked, "Is there something oozing out of it? And does it itch?" Rosina said yes to both questions.

"It's a chigger bite. Wait a minute, and I'll get something for it," I said, as I turned toward the front door.

Claudia Clavel

When I returned with a bottle of red nail polish, they all stared at me in silence. I dabbed it on her bite and pulled up my shirt to reveal my own chigger bite, with a bright red spot on top. We were all laughing as Rosina backed down our driveway.

The following week, the same car drove up for more advice. After the usual formal greeting, Rosina held out her arm and said, "Look, it's gone. You fixed it." She went on, "I urinate all the time. What's wrong with me?"

By then, I was feeling real concern, not for how often the woman urinated, but that she thought I was a *curandera*, or healer. While collecting my thoughts, I asked Rosina how many sodas she drank during the day. She replied, "Six or seven." I explained about caffeine being a diuretic, and the need to replace it with water, but I could tell that wasn't what she wanted to hear.

Then I launched into my defense, explaining that I was not a *curandera* and didn't know much about medical conditions, except for practical things. I told her our daughter was a nurse, so I knew medical terminology, but could not heal. The women in the car all nodded and seemed to understand. That was the last time anyone came to me to be healed. However, it did alert us to the concept of being labeled through some abstract association known only to our neighbors.

As people grew to know us, we began to hire someone now and then to help with things we didn't know how to do. The first thing we needed help with was the metal west roof overhang. It needed to be extended over the walk that ran along that side of the house. We hired Claudio Tafoya for the job and were amused when his wife, Rosina, and three daughters showed up every afternoon as well, to sit in the shade and watch him work. It was Claudio and Rosina who asked why our house was so "fresh" (cool) during the heat of the day.

Accidental Anthropologists

We told them that we opened all the doors and windows at night to cool things off. It was then they noticed the screens on our doors and windows. Rosina said, "Aren't you afraid of the Drinkers? Or the 'night air'?"

Thomas and I tried to assure them we weren't afraid of being bothered by the Drinkers (more about them later). Then I asked about "night air": "Why are you concerned about the air at night?"

We were informed that "night air" could make us sick, and that was one of the reasons why people never opened their doors or windows at night. It took us a while to figure that one out, but then we connected mosquitoes with "night air" and *mal aria*: Spanish for bad air. Our neighbors hadn't seemed to make that connection, so they thought it was just night air that could make them sick. Thomas and I explained the malaria connection to Claudio and his wife, and the next thing we knew, the couple came to ask whether we might have extra screens for their windows.

We had recently bought two hundred assorted aluminum frame windows and one hundred screens from a lumber store in Santa Fe that was discontinuing the line. We paid $125 for the lot and became the talk of the lumberyard, as I made trip after trip to load them into our little truck. We did give Claudio and Rosina screens, and Thomas taught Claudio how to take the aluminum frames apart and cut them to fit their windows. Word soon spread, as others showed up for screens and lessons.

Over the years, we used all those windows for various projects, and neighbors laughed as they watched them become one thing and then another. Thomas soon had a reputation for dismantling and reassembling all sorts of building materials. We didn't know it at the time, but that was a way of life for most folks in the area. Over the years, we had been astounded by the ingenuity and creativity of our neighbors. It was the perfect environment for the two of us.

5

Perfecto and Pilar Garcia

The first person Thomas and I became acquainted with was Perfecto Garcia, postmaster of the little San Ignacio post office. He had recently replaced Graciela Roybal, who retired after serving many years as postmistress. At that time, Graciela's original grocery store served as the post office. There was a divider consisting of individual mailboxes and a counter that separated the room into two sections. Stepping through the old screen door with a bread advertisement stenciled on the front made you feel good about going for the mail. There was something warm and inviting about that space. Graciela wasn't as outgoing as Perfecto, so we didn't know her very well, but she was a very nice lady and was looking forward to retirement after thirty years. He replaced her shortly after we moved into the village.

It wasn't too long before the U.S. Postal Service began to replace all the small village home post offices with manufactured buildings. They came completely ready to do business shortly after they were set up. The day the new post office rolled into the tunnel beneath the highway, Perfecto's excitement grew. However, it wasn't an easy entrance. About halfway in, the new post office got stuck in the tunnel. It wouldn't budge. It was being hauled on a long flatbed trailer, so Donilio Vigil suggested they let air out of the trailer tires, hoping there would be enough clearance to squeeze through.

That was tried, but to no avail. Herculano thought they should back the trailer out of the tunnel and take it the long way around the village on a rutted dirt road that ran through state land.

The delivery driver must have chuckled, as all the village men were able to get the very modern post office delivered to its destination the hard way. However, it did take a while. A client had come by our place to pick up a tee shirt order and wound up staying for dinner when he couldn't get out through the tunnel. Several hours went by before the tunnel was cleared.

Perfecto laughed about his wife being our Neighborhood Watch security, for she spent every morning cruising in her car to check out the new building. It was parked in front of Graciela's house until the foundation and septic system were installed. Perfecto had worried about vandalism but that never happened.

Our new postmaster loved people, so he was the perfect fit for the job. He was very friendly and generous to a fault. When anyone in the valley had a problem, they made their way to the post office, and Perfecto. I don't think the man ever turned anyone away who was in real need. Over the years, I watched the postmaster pull bills out of his pocket to support endless school fund-raisers. He could never turn down a bag of *calabacitos* a neighbor had just picked from their garden or a basket of apples from someone's tree, when they were in need of a few dollars. It worked that way in the valley. It was a collective cultural agreement among people of limited means.

Everybody understood that if each person chipped in a few bucks, it would add up to enough money to help

Accidental Anthropologists

a neighbor in need. It was the same with weddings, funerals, birthdays and graduations. A traditional "money tree" served as the vehicle at some events. Dollar bills were pinned to the clothing of newlyweds during the wedding dance, to help start their new life. Alternatively, in the case of a funeral or serious illness, large jars were set on counters of local businesses, with names of the family noted. Neighbors gave whatever they could afford to help the family of the suffering or deceased.

Sometimes, money was simply needed to help with gas when a person had to drive the eighty-mile round trip to the city for chemo or physical therapy. It took some time for us to learn that there was a specific amount of money allotted for each event. Perfecto helped us sort it all out, and we were happy to become a part of the tradition. It was a very simple form of social welfare that continues to this day.

When Perfecto wasn't busy, people, including the Drinkers, congregated in the lobby and stood quietly until he was free. More than once, I witnessed a small group of neighbors standing together, waiting for their postmaster to engage in social conversation. It was there that I noticed a very different Spanish dialect from what I had heard in the Chula Vista valley. The lilt was missing. San Ignacio Spanish came from a place deeper in the throat, and it was filled with constantly changing idioms, making it nearly impossible for outsiders to understand. Thomas and I both spoke Spanish but we never understood the local version.

In northern New Mexico, Spanglish was considered a second language. Sometimes, every other word was in English. People had that down to a science, as the speaker flew through a sentence, weaving in and out of languages. Not too long after I noticed the difference in dialects, I vis-

Claudia Clavel

ited a local woman in Valle Chico, a village at the southern end of the valley. Piedad had just poured us cups of coffee when her phone rang. The conversation was in Spanish, and in response to a question, I heard her say, *"No, Ella es un Americana."* By then, it was pretty clear that Thomas and I had stumbled into a foreign world.

Perfecto heard all the valley gossip, and he offered useful advice on just about any subject. You could present him with a question or request for about anything under the sun. Within a few days, whatever you happened to need turned up at your door. The village postmaster was a conduit for the entire valley. All in all, Perfecto was one nice guy. After he retired, the post office was never quite the same, and Perfecto often said he missed the role he had played in San Ignacio. Most of us felt the same.

Pilar was Perfecto's wife. Early on, the two of us became acquainted because of apple butter. Shortly after moving into our little adobe, we were visited by a family of five out-of-state friends for a two-week stay. We had figured out the sleeping logistics but didn't have a kitchen table to gather around for meals. We had six unfinished chairs that I had designed but not completed. At least they were useable. The logical thing to do was to ask Perfecto for guidance. Sure enough, that evening he drove up to our place with a dining table in the back of his truck. Perfecto said it was an old one he found in their storage room.

At the end of our friends' visit, we returned the table to its owners and thanked them for their generosity I took five jars of homemade jam, three of them apple butter. That's when we met Pilar. A few days later at the post office, Perfecto said to me, "Claudia, my wife said to ask if you would teach her how to make apple butter. The whole family loved it."

Accidental Anthropologists

"Sure," I replied. "It's easy to make. Just let me know when you get some apples." A week or so later, Perfecto told me they had apples from a relative's tree down the valley.

The next day, I loaded my big pans into the car and drove to Pilar's to begin the apple butter project. We worked all morning peeling and cutting apples. I left Pilar to stir the apple puree and returned the next morning to fill the jars and get them in a water bath for canning. Over the two-day period of sharing a pleasurable task, Pilar told me about her illness: she had suffered a brain aneurism the year before our arrival. The woman had gone into a coma, and the doctors hadn't held out much hope for her recovery. Pilar's family and all the villages up and down the valley prayed constantly for her. Perfecto and their five children visited Pilar at the hospital twice a day to sit with her and pray.

Five months later, unexpectedly, Pilar woke up and became the miracle of the valley. According to Perfecto, before his wife's illness, she had been full of fun and laughter, always the life of the party. When I met Pilar, she seemed flat, almost morose, given to abrupt bursts of commentary. When she addressed her daughter, Cristilina, it sounded like a barking command.

It took me a while to get used to Pilar's verbal style, as we continued cooking on a weekly basis. A doctor had recently told my neighbor she needed to be on a low-fat diet, and Pilar didn't know where to begin. She asked if I would help her, and I agreed to get started, so we continued our cooking dates for several more weeks. During that time, we became better acquainted, and I became more at ease with her abrupt style.

One day, Pilar told me that since her illness, she had been reluctant to make contact with old friends. It was the same with many relatives, who longed to have her back in their lives. Pilar's Hispanic culture was based on close family and friendship ties, and her absence had caused a lot of heartache among both groups, especially when everyone had been praying for her recovery all those months. It was as though she had come back, but not to them.

Pilar and I talked about that for some time. Finally, I told her I thought it would be good for her physical and mental wellbeing if she could bring herself to call some of those people. However, she said she felt embarrassed by her illness. She was afraid people would laugh at her. I told her I thought people were probably crying over their feelings of loss.

The next time Pilar and I met, I was greeted with a big hug. My friend had the biggest smile on her face. She said, "Claudia, I think God sent you to me. Not only have I learned to make apple butter and other things, but you showed me how to get back to my family and friends."

My brave friend had gathered all her strength, picked up the phone and called the people who loved her. I nearly fell over from surprise and delight, for I understood the courage it took for Pilar to make those calls. By the beginning of the next year, Perfecto and Pilar became *mayordomos* for the church once again. Every year the role was rotated throughout the village. The next thing we knew, Pilar was out on the fiesta circuit, recruiting people to work and gathering donations of food and white elephant items. Perfecto and I laughed as we visualized our neighbors trying to hold back from the formidable woman. Pilar went on to become the best recruiter/fundraiser in the valley.

Over the years, Pilar and I occasionally cooked together, usually in the fall, when someone had given us

Accidental Anthropologists

pumpkins from their garden. The size of the pumpkins determined how creative we became, but we could always count on pumpkin rolls, for that was the focus, with Thanksgiving in mind. Sometimes we spent six or seven hours in my kitchen, whipping up the rolls, mini-breads and pumpkin cookies. Pilar's family became addicted to the fruit of our labors. We have enjoyed revisiting those scenes, with the heavenly aroma of spices in the overheated kitchen air.

From the day Pilar made her phone calls, she wanted to do something for me. She would call me to ask whether she might be able to help me with some task. I was such a loner, and especially so with my art, I just couldn't think of anything—except for one time. Pilar was always concerned with how hard I worked in my studio, so she asked if there wasn't some tedious chore she could help me with, or maybe just sit with me while I worked to keep me company. In her world, people didn't like to be alone, and village folks thought it odd that Thomas and I preferred solitude. I knew I had to come up with something, so Pilar could stop worrying about repaying me.

At the time, I was working on a complex collage that required over a thousand little pieces of torn paper. To convince her of the absolute boredom required of my art, I said to her, "Okay, if you want to tear paper for me, come tomorrow."

My friend was delighted and relieved to be of some service. Pilar arrived promptly at nine the next morning, and we sat in my studio, tearing painted red paper into little pieces. I put on some classical music, and for three hours, we sat and tore paper, hardly saying a word.

At the end of the shift, Pilar stood up, stretched, and said, "That's the most boring thing I've ever done in my life." A funny statement from a woman who could sit for hours, peeling thirty-pound sacks of roasted chiles. We went in for lunch, and Pilar added, "I don't ever want to do that again." I knew then that her debt to me had been settled.

Pilar and I continued our friendship throughout the years. I grew to enjoy her ironic sense of humor and to marvel at her heroic efforts to make big dietary changes in their life after she was diagnosed with diabetes. Perfecto and Pilar's daughter had become a dietician, and she guided her mother in new ways of cooking the traditional Spanish foods. Pilar's doctors were amazed and impressed by her determination to make things better. In addition, I have always wondered, "Who got sent to whom?"

6

The Drinkers

One of the dangerous reputations of the village when we moved in had to do with a group of guys who spent their days drinking and doing drugs. Most of the men at that time were Vietnam veterans living on SSI or military disability pensions. A few others were jobless, surviving on whatever they could scrounge amongst their friends and family. Heroin was a major influence in some of their lives. Alcoholism was shared by all of them. The Drinkers pretty much dominated the place and cast a pall over the village.

For some reason, that awareness didn't daunt us. Thomas and I were too involved with our own survival, we were kind of off to the side by ourselves, and the trouble had taken over the center of the village. There were around ten or more Drinkers, as everyone referred to them, and they had all been born in San Ignacio and were related to everyone, so they were woven into the fabric of the place. People gave them rides if they were walking toward La Tienda or a bar in the opposite direction. When they needed to go to town, the Drinkers paid people for rides. Most often, they walked the mile to La Cantina to meet with old friends for beer and a game of pool. It was all the walking that kept some of them alive into old age.

Claudia Clavel

From the beginning, we hired one or another of the Drinkers when we had any spare cash. Most were great woodchoppers and not afraid of hard manual labor. They watched us, and how hard we worked, and over time, we gained their respect. We also paid them a bit more than the locals did. The minimum wage was quite a bit lower than it was where we had come from, so we had a different view of earned money. It probably helped that there were always baked goods to be shared with a cup of coffee at the end of a work session. Thomas and I were good listeners, and the Drinkers liked to tell their stories, so that became a bond for us. Over time, Thomas and I grew to admire the Drinkers' humor. A joke was only dark if the occasion called for it; otherwise, it was simple, topical and hilarious. One of my favorite stories was about Preciliano's dog eating his cordless phone.

A few years after our arrival, on a sunny summer morning our phone was ringing as I entered the kitchen. It was a neighbor calling with a request: he asked whether we might have an extra cordless telephone that we could pass on to Preciliano Medina. Lorenzo started laughing as he began the story of how the man's dog had eaten his phone. Then he grew serious as he told me that Preciliano was waiting for a call from someone interested in helping him with his manuscripts. The whole village was hoping for that to happen, so the telephone replacement seemed urgent.

I made a call to Thomas at work, to see whether he might have an old cordless phone lying around the shop. While I waited, he rummaged through desk drawers, and, as fate would have it, found one left behind by a former work-study student. I called Lorenzo back with the good news and told him Thomas would deliver the phone to Preciliano on his way home from work.

Accidental Anthropologists

When Thomas drove up to Preciliano's house, there were several guys sitting in a row in the shade, drinking beer. After handshakes all around, somebody handed Thomas a beer, and he passed the cordless phone to Preciliano. Thomas asked him if the dog had actually swallowed his phone, and before the dog owner could answer, the jokes started flying.

One guy wondered, "Could you hear the phone ring if it was in the dog's stomach? And would you have to hold the dog up to your ear to answer?" Albino went on, "How could you dial?" and Thomas quipped, "The dialing buttons light up, so maybe they would show up through the skin on the dog's stomach. If so, you tell the dog to roll over, and press in the numbers."

Ambrosio asked, "Which end would you talk into?" and Urbano Ortega replied, "I know this much, if you lift the tail to answer, you will know it's a telemarketer."

Thomas spent about an hour with the group, and they kept the jokes going and never stopped laughing over the saga. It was a topic in the village for a few days, as others contributed to the line of jokes. It was never determined whether the dog actually swallowed the phone, and by then it didn't matter, for the story itself had become great entertainment. It was a true Shaggy Dog story.

Up until the Second World War, the population of San Ignacio had been around 2,000 inhabitants. By the time we arrived, that number had dropped to 100 souls. The war had drained most of the rural areas in New Mexico as young men went off to serve their country. When they returned from the battlefields, with the G.I. Bill offering education and help with housing, most found a better life in cities across the country. Villages like

Claudia Clavel

San Ignacio languished for years. Thomas and I used to laugh, watching network TV weather forecasters, for they always stood in front of New Mexico when a map of the country came up. That's probably one of the reasons New Mexico earned the title: One of Our Fifty Is Missing.

Over the years, we met a number of people who had come to places like San Ignacio all over the state during the 1970s. The "Back to the Land" movement was taking place, and it was the main reason Thomas and I had pulled up stakes and headed to northern New Mexico. One of the problems during that era stemmed from the free-living style of the Anglo invaders. More than one neighbor told us that the hippies' behavior became so intolerable in the village that someone set a hippie's car on fire and sent him walking barefoot out of the village. After that, most of the other Anglo outsiders filtered away, leaving the villages in peace once more. The local people had never had a problem with who moved into their area, as long as they didn't try to impose their values or judgments on them.

The Drinkers had returned from their war to a very different situation. The village was the same as it had been before they left. However, they were not. The men simply didn't know how to fix themselves, so they hung out together and self-medicated. And told their stories to anyone who would listen to them. Early on, the Drinkers realized that Thomas and I were listening, and a very interesting thing happened. Within a rather short time, most of the men became protective of us, and one of them came to us to say that we would never be bothered by anyone as long as we lived in the village. After thirty years, that has been the case.

One sharply cold winter day, something new showed up on the plaza, and it had the entire village chuckling. It was an old, beat-up, red-and-white school bus with an Activity Bus sign on the front. It belonged to our neighbor Lorenzo Garcia. He parked the bus at the end of our driveway, and we used it as a landmark when directing people to our place. Lorenzo used it to ferry the Drinkers to and from the bars during the morning hours in winter. He drove no more than 10 miles an hour, and his passengers loved going that slowly. They called it "cruising." During the afternoons, Lorenzo parked his Activity Bus on the plaza, and the Drinkers piled in to socialize and drink in the warmth of the afternoon sun. They called it "solarizing." And one of them always hollered out to passersby, "Hey, hop on for a beer."

There was a huge house on the plaza, enclosed by a high adobe wall. The guy who lived there was a prison guard at the state pen in Santa Fe. During his time off, he played host to the Drinkers. When we walked to the post office, we could often hear the festivities as the wind carried their music and voices over the wall into the plaza.

Around that time, there was a big prison break in Santa Fe, with six or seven escapees loose. They weren't caught for a couple of weeks, and we always thought there were several of them in that party house. We heard whooping and laughter, day and night, as the party went on continuously for two weeks.

During the prison break, our son-in-law and grandson were visiting. As we were driving them to the airport, we were stopped by a State Police roadblock. At that time, they were still looking for the escaped convicts. A police officer approached our car, and Thomas rolled his window down and then heard, "Hey Thomas, where you headed?" It was our neighbor Eusebio Medina. What a surprise. We didn't know he was a cop. Because we were neighbors, we had to chat for a moment about the escape.

Claudia Clavel

Thomas did say, "Maybe you need to check out the house on the plaza. There's been a party going on since the break." Eusebio laughed and said, "Man, there's always a party going on at that house."

Our son-in-law and grandson were amazed that we would know someone in a police roadblock. But it was that kind of place then, with the population of the state just a million and a half. It was not uncommon to bump into many people with connections to the area. Thomas stopped one time on his way to work to take off his sweater, and two cars immediately pulled up behind him to see if he needed help. He knew both drivers casually, but if people recognized you or your car, then you were known. That happened frequently over the years, and it was another reason the Drinkers were able to get around. If you broke down, you didn't have to stick out your thumb or raise the hood of your car to get someone's attention.

7

Tea Party Girls

Once we were settled in and began meeting more neighbors, I noticed there were many young children in the village. We had met the three little Archuleta girls when their dad worked on our roof. At the time, we thought it odd that Claudio brought his wife and children to work with him, but we were new to the village, so what did we know about people's work habits? It was summer, and hot, so I took iced mint tea to the family and sat with them for a while, chatting about life in San Ignacio. The girls were seven, four and three, shy, quiet and well behaved. They would sit for hours, waiting for their dad to finish his work. Some days Claudio came later, but always with the family in tow.

It was during that time that the ritual of afternoon tea took hold. It had been my habit for many years to have afternoon tea around four o'clock. If the Archuleta family was still around at three, I simply moved teatime up and invited them in to sit at our table. Baking was big in my life back then, so there was always a dessert, and I especially loved sharing food with people. The girls were amused when I handed them floral cloth napkins and teacups on saucers. They giggled a lot but seemed to enjoy it all. At the time, I didn't know the impact that afternoon tea would have on that family and later, on the village.

Claudia Clavel

A few years after Claudio had finished the roof job, his daughter Maya came up with a couple of friends to sell us school raffle tickets. She asked to show her friends around the house, especially the bathroom, where a Mexican box filled with wooden skeletons sat on a stand next to the john. You could make the skeletons move their arms and legs and some of them sit up out of their coffins when you turned a little handle on the side of the box. That Mexican box had always been a favorite with children. As the girls were getting ready to leave, Crystal, one of the friends, asked if they could come again to visit. Before I could answer, Maya replied, "Well, you should come when we have tea time." I had to smile at the child's sureness, for it was a great idea, and I should have thought of it myself.

Word traveled fast, so it didn't take long before our neighbors were hearing about afternoon tea at Claudia's house. On a summer morning, I found a group of little girls waiting for me outside the post office. Nina Archuleta, the least shy of the group, spoke up, "Claudia, these other girls want to know about mint tea. I told them they should go to your house and try some." It was that simple. I told them we would have a tea party, and they could invite anyone they wanted to come. We set a date, but I told them someone had to call me a day or two ahead with the number of guests who would be coming.

Maya was six years old by then, and I knew her well enough to ask if she would help me with the guest list. Thomas printed invitations for us, and my new assistant took on the role of distributing the invitations. What I didn't know was that Maya invited only those girls she liked. A couple of girls were left out, and I heard from their mothers. From the get-go, I had to coach my young assistant in the fine art of diplomacy.

Accidental Anthropologists

It didn't take long for Maya to become quite professional in her role. The child would present me with a list of all the girls who had received invitations, and she made a practice of phoning me the day before the party with a guest count, so planning became quite easy for me.

Since Maya was taking the tea party project so seriously, I decided the tea parties themselves had to be presented professionally. Those were lean years for us financially, but I managed to find colorful and festive paper plates, cups, napkins and tablecloths at a discount store. I squeezed out enough cash to buy a bouquet of fresh flowers and a small bag of mixed bulk candy to strew down the center of the table. One time I cut shapes out of watermelon slices and stuck wooden skewers in the upside-down watermelon end, so the cut shapes became melon pops. I always baked a layer cake that was highly decorated and served on a pedestal plate.

On one occasion, I lined little clay flowerpots with foil and layered instant chocolate and vanilla pudding inside. A flower-shaped sucker was stuck in the chocolate layer. All that, because I had bought six packs of marigolds to actually plant in the pots, but the flowers turned out to be larger than the containers. On that tea party day, the little girls filed into our summerhouse and stopped in their tracks at the sight of the festive table. Their eyes lit up as they took their seats and settled in for tea. The flowerpots were a big hit.

Since choosing different teas had become a part of our tea ritual, I decided to serve four kinds. Over time, I had introduced the children to licorice mint, peppermint, spearmint and their favorite, jasmine. A potter friend had given me two teapots, and I had a couple of cheap ones. I filled all four on party days. I also made a big pitcher of iced hibiscus tea, because the doll-size teacups didn't provide much liquid for washing down cake. My tea party guests drank all the choices, and table conversation generally included who liked what the best. After so much tea, there would soon be a line to the bathroom. A big part of the trip was to have a turn at the handle on the skeleton box.

The children were always on their best behavior, even the little two- and three-year-olds. I sat with them and always initiated the conversations, for they were very shy. One year we invited the moms, and it was a disaster. There wasn't enough room for the moms in the summerhouse, and they didn't want to intrude, so they sat in the shade of the house. I ran back and forth serving, and then realized the girls were upset that I was not sitting with them. They let their moms know that they would not be invited again.

Our first tea party was always in June, when we had a big rosebush covered with Red Blaze roses. Sometimes I picked blooms to float in a huge, low ceramic bowl for the center of the table. One year, little Venus said, "My mom loves roses," and I replied, "Well, why don't we take some to her. I have a big pan and we'll put some water in and float them to her." I wound up driving the girls home, each with a pan of water on her lap, covered with red roses. It took several trips, and I had to drive very slowly on the back roads due to all the potholes. That was an once-in-a-lifetime offer.

One summer, our daughter Julie was visiting from California, and it coincided with our tea party, so she jumped right in. Julie turned out to be a big hit when she offered to read tea leaves for the girls. They had to clean out their tiny cups because of the layers of sugar that had built up after so many choices. Julie managed to capture the guests' complete attention as she moved from cup to cup, telling each child's fortune. The group was hanging on every word. That event was still being talked about many years later.

Boys sat in on our tea parties every now and then, but they never quite took to it like the girls. It was interesting to observe interactions among the children when that occurred. The boys didn't tease the girls, and the girls didn't giggle about having boys present. I could tell they were all enjoying the tea party experience. Children in the village were close and played together, especially in summer when the big activity was swimming in the river.

Once they hit puberty, age became an entirely different story. Teenagers, especially the girls, generally withdrew from their previous lives as children and seemed more withdrawn and reclusive, especially so around adults outside their family unit. I had to remind myself to approach teen girls at village gatherings because they had become so shy and hesitant, even after all the years of tea parties.

One hot June afternoon there was a tea party, when the second-generation girls were in their early teens, and one boy joined the group. He was about ten years old at the time, and became so disruptive that the girls asked me to make him leave. In more than twenty years, that was the only time I ever witnessed a tea party kerfuffle.

For a few years, we had one tea party in summer and one during Christmas break, weather permitting. One winter party, I served hot chocolate with a candy cane for stirring. Since it was holiday time, the girls turned up in party attire, and I was horrified to see red candy cane juice dripping down the fronts of a few dresses. We didn't make that mistake again.

Another favorite event for the children occurred when our friend Douglas asked to be part of the party. He was the potter who had made my teapots. Douglas also worked for a catering company at the time and had been a captain for a while, so he suggested that he be the waiter and tea server. He was a tall, handsome guy with a lot of charm, and he stood next to the teapots with a white tea towel draped over one arm, waiting for an order. The girls ordered all right. They ran the waiter ragged with endless requests of multiple choices, and they giggled throughout the entire event.

In 2006, I suffered a ruptured disk and spent a long time convalescing. When June rolled around, I was still in no shape to clean out the summerhouse and pull off a tea party. A group of little girls was waiting for me outside the post office one afternoon. They asked when the party would be held. I told them my back hadn't recovered fully, so we would have to wait until it healed. No one said anything for a while. They just stood quietly looking at me. Finally, Katrina spoke up, "We'll come and clean the summerhouse for you." Then others chimed in, "Yeah, we can do all the work. We will set the table and decorate, and do everything. We can even pick the roses."

By that time, the children were second-generation tea party girls, most of them around five or six years old. Mariah was three. Sure enough, a little army of children showed up at our door shortly after our meeting and took over. I had to laugh as I watched them haul pillows and *banco* covers onto the patio to beat out the dust. Nina and Maya polished the table and window ledges with lemon oil. Katrina led a group of three little ones who washed windows and swept the floor. Venus could barely reach the window but went at it with gusto. The girls came back the next day to decorate the table and then they picked red roses to float in the big ceramic bowl. We were ready for a tea party.

Accidental Anthropologists

One summer, I asked Helga Schultz, a German abstract painter friend if she would like to share a few small paintings with the girls and talk about what it was like to paint something so different from reality. Helga had retired from teaching art history at a university. She began her talk in a heavy German accent, launching into a college-level lecture on abstract painting. The roomful of girls sat completely still, their eyes on the artist. With nary a peep, it appeared as though they were fully engaged in the lecture. On the other hand, I was having a quiet fit, as the artist droned on and on. Finally, I stood and thanked Helga for coming and said something about the ice cream melting and needing to get on with the party. After she left, I thanked the girls for being so patient and asked them what they thought of abstract art. The consensus among the group: they hadn't understood a word the artist said, or her paintings.

The tea parties went on for many years, until the girls became teenagers and more withdrawn. Some time later, when the village gathered for a funeral dinner, I found myself seated across from Erica and Emmi. Both girls had been tea party regulars. Erica was about to graduate from high school, and Emmi was a freshman in college. Erica's mom and Emmi's grandma were sitting next to me. Rosina said, "Claudia, the girls were hoping you would be here. They said it's been a long time since they have been to your house." I looked at the two near-adults and said, "I thought you had outgrown tea parties. I hardly ever see you now that you are all grown up. So, are you interested in having a tea party?" Erica quickly replied, "We thought you would never ask. And our moms would like to come too."

8

Diego

My first awareness of Diego occurred when I saw him with his mother, sitting on a rock alongside the road behind their house. Cassandra was holding his infant sister, Adela, in her arms and watching a mare being bred in the corral across the road from them. I remember smiling, thinking how different life was in a village. Cassandra and Alfredo Rodriguez moved into the village the year after we bought our place. It was a while before we became acquainted, so Diego was probably around two years old when we first met, and his half-brother, Aaron, was a little over four.

From the very beginning, Diego came to visit if he saw me outdoors working in the yard. No matter what chore I was doing, the child fell in beside me. I was usually pulling weeds or picking rocks and bits of broken glass out of the dried earth. At first, I worried that Diego was too young to be messing with broken glass, but then Thomas reminded me that children here grow up surrounded by hazardous materials: rusty nails, spikes, old boards, bits of rusted tin roofing and broken glass everywhere. Our first year in San Ignacio, we hauled five pickup loads of rusted tin cans and broken glass off the hill. For umpteen years, people had been heaving their trash out their backdoors and into the surrounding open space. Breaking beer bottles and pop bottles remained a recreational pastime.

During the early years, when Thomas and I shared studio space, Diego spent time with one or both of us on a daily basis while we worked. Usually, the little boy came for an hour or so in the morning and then again in the afternoon. My end of the shop consisted of a worktable and a crude bookshelf for my supplies. I kept a paper punch, child scissors, and a little stack of scrap paper on a shelf near where Diego sat on a little stool. He would sit quietly, punching holes in little pieces of paper or cutting paper into shapes. With the three of us engrossed in our work, we never needed chatter in order to spend time together. Thomas and I used to laugh when, after an hour or so, the child would suddenly stand up, put everything away in its place and announce, "I'm going now. Bye." He maintained that abrupt behavior into adulthood.

Diego never grew very much. He was a tiny, almost miniature little boy, remaining so as each year passed. He had a big appetite, so his parents were concerned. A doctor told them tonsils might be the problem, but the little boy was too young to have them removed. Sadly, his family soon fell apart, and that surgery never happened. Thomas and I cannot remember Diego ever being sick. He was extremely mellow and quiet, and very curious about the world around him. He constantly asked questions about things that interested him and was unusually open about experiencing anything new, especially when it came to food.

Diego's diet at home consisted almost entirely of beans, chile, potatoes, and, of course, flour tortillas. However, the child became visually excited at the prospect of trying something new, perhaps an avocado or an artichoke. Or just about anything I happened to be fixing when he was with us. If it was a combination of foods, such as a casserole or soup, Diego wanted to know about each ingredient. Early on, his interest and curiosity were most sincere. The child was like a sponge; he soaked up as much information as possible outside his known world. I listened to classical music a good portion of each day, so Diego was exposed to that every time he was with us. One day when he about four, he asked, "What kind of music is that?" I replied, "It's called classical music, and most of it was written a long, long time ago." His response was, "Hmm, nice."

Diego was around that same age when I was digging a lot of holes for planting flowers and vegetables. Hole digging had become a Zen experience for me, simply because it required hours and hours of patient time, extracting rocks of every size and shape. I could dig a slight depression using a shovel, but then it required a crowbar or piece of rebar to chisel and lift each rock out of the slowly emerging opening. By the time the hole had been excavated, a pile of rocks bigger than the hole stood nearby.

On one of those occasions, Diego strolled up to see what I was doing. Without a word, the little boy found another piece of rebar and began unearthing stones. Each time he lifted a rock out of the ground, he held it in his hands and talked to it. The conversation went something like this: "Look at this poor guy, he's mad because I took him out of his warm bed. Now he is mad because I'm taking him away from his family. I'd better put them all in the same pile, so they can be together." Diego always gave the stones gender and held each one in his hand a while, pondering the impact of his unearthing.

Claudia Clavel

Digging holes was never quite the same for me after that. The little boy and I dug up rocks together for several years, until he and his family moved away. Thomas had taken a full-time job in Santa Teresa around the same time, so I was left alone much of the day. By then, I had my own studio and was fully engaged in making art, so never bored. However, I did miss Diego. He had become so much a part of my daily life, the loss was apparent immediately.

It was then that I noticed the rhythm of our time together: during winter and the cold months, Diego entered the world of my studio or kitchen. We spent time quietly together, he engaged in punching holes or cutting paper into shapes while I cooked or worked on a collage or drawing. When the weather warmed, we moved outdoors, delighted to be at work with the sun warming our backs. I hadn't realized how much we accomplished together until after he moved away. Many of my garden areas were a direct result of unearthing Diego's many stone friends.

From the time they were very young, our three grandsons spent part of their summers with us. One fall, we had Alex and Tyler for six weeks, when they were two and five years old. Diego was still living down below us then, so he became a regular fixture in our household during that time. From then on, every summer until their teens, our grandsons and Diego became inseparable. The city boys and their country friend whiled away the days of summer, expanding their boundaries with each passing year. At first, they rarely left the hill, but eventually they climbed through the barbed-wire fence to set up life on the huge rock formations just above the arroyo behind my studio. Diego's father was a carpenter, and that skill seemed to come naturally to his son. He was constantly instructing the other boys in some building project. We never seemed at a loss for old lumber, so the children had an ample supply to draw from, year after year.

One summer, we had all three grandsons; Andrew, Tyler and Alex for six weeks. Diego was seven at the time and came up with the idea of making adobe bricks as a group project. He included Aaron and their cousins, Ines and Damian, who lived down the road from us. That brought the number of children to seven. Diego divided them into teams of workers, with himself as supervisor. He had learned the art of adobe making from his father and knew the process.

Thomas and I laughed aloud as we observed the youthful group seriously engaged in their tasks. Alex and Damian, both age three, struggled to carry a bucket half full of water from the spigot to the mud hole, where Diego stood waiting with a hoe. Tyler, along with Andrew, Ines and Aaron, hauled armloads of straw to be worked into the adobe clay. They took turns stomping straw into the mud with their feet, shrieking and laughing as the cold mud squished up between their toes.

Diego constructed an adobe mold from four pieces of scrap lumber, and the boys all helped to pack the mud into the mold. Diego told them the bricks had to rest for a while before being turned out on the hard-packed ground to dry in the sun. The children labored at the task for most of the day, with nary a squabble. I was always amazed at how well they all got along. Our grandsons shared a kindness to others with the local boys. During all our years, Thomas and I witnessed that same consideration consistently among the children of the area.

The river had always been a focal point of summer life, even for us adults in the village. Thomas and I spent many a scorching summer afternoon jumping in the river to cool off. We used to laugh with our neighbors that it was an organic form of air-conditioning. Diego's ease with river life came as a mixed bag of blessings, especially in the early years, when the children had to be watched for their own good. It was hard to convince Andrew, Tyler and Alex that they couldn't run off to play in the river with Diego as their responsible caretaker. They had to learn to wait until Grandpa Thomas got home from work, and then they could go for their evening water adventure.

A highlight occurred one full moon night, when Thomas took the boys to the river just as it was growing dark. The five of them lined up in the mud, sitting in water up to their chins, just in time for the bats to come out for their evening hunting expedition. There were many mosquitoes then, so plenty to feed the darting, diving swarm. The bats flew inches from their faces, and I could hear shrieks of terror and delight drifting up from the river below.

Day after summer day, Diego led our grandsons into one adventure after the other. They traveled the arroyo maze in back of the house where they found arrowheads and pottery shards. He taught them to skin a snake and tack it on a board to dry. We bought all the boys feathered headdresses and little tomahawks and for two summers, they became Indians. With some assistance from their grandpa, the four of them constructed slingshots, bows, and arrows for rabbit-hunting forays. They wore loincloths and wandered around the hilltop and arroyos with their bows and arrows, giving each other menacing looks. We never had a rabbit to cook but did eat our share of trout.

It seemed like overnight the boys lost interest in forts and all things Indian. For the next few summers, fishing became their passion. Once again, Diego was the source of information, for he knew all about hooks, lines, and appropriate bait. He also knew the very best fishing holes along our stretch of river. The first summer Tyler and Alex were allowed to fish without an adult, our daughter Julie, their mother, was here. The two of us were a bit nervous about the boys wandering the river without adult supervision. But, we did want them to have the experience, so common among the village children. Julie and I packed them a bag of snacks, and, with Diego in the lead; off they went, down our hill and across the plaza toward the river.

We watched them from the driveway until they reached the curve in the road just past the post office. My daughter and I looked at one another, each feeling a little fear mixed with amazement that they were off on their own. About every hour or so, without mentioning our fears, Julie and I took turns driving down to the fishing hole with bottles of hibiscus tea to drink or another snack. The boys were delighted with all the attention and rewarded us with enough trout for supper.

During one of Julie's deliveries, Diego convinced her that it was safe for the boys to jump off the old bridge into the river. He had already scouted the area, making sure the water was deep enough. Julie went through a number of emotions before she could bring herself to give permission. She told me later that it was a grand moment for her sons, for the bridge was high above the water. At that time, Alex was seven, Tyler ten, and Diego eleven. It was a true adventure for them.

During the monsoon rains, the river depth was never consistent. Sometimes, sand from the arroyos was carried into the swimming holes by torrents of water coursing down from the top of the mesa. Other times, the deposited sand was scoured out by an even bigger storm.

Claudia Clavel

It was Diego, who jumped off all the high points, including the burned bridge. He would show us adults and the village children where it was safe to jump into the water. Into adulthood, he remained one of the most daring and devil-may-care human beings we had ever known. As time passed, that would prove to be his downfall.

If Diego wasn't with our grandsons, he was out alone, scouting the river and arroyos. He was happiest wandering around the valley, exploring. After he moved to Ojo de Vaca with his family, the boy walked three miles to our place in the summers, using the river or railroad tracks as his route.

As the children grew older, each summer presented new and more exciting adventures. Diego was always at the center of any activity. Our grandsons lived in cities, and it would take at least a week for them to slow down and mellow to the rhythm of life in the country. Surprisingly, for years after Diego moved out of the village, the child would turn up the day before our grandsons' arrival. We never knew exactly when they might get here, for it was never a fixed date. Thomas and I always wondered how Diego knew they were about to arrive. Pretty much from the day the boys showed up, Diego moved in with us and stayed until they left. Thomas and I moved out of the house and into my studio upstairs guest room. The downstairs was turned into a boys' dorm, and for the duration of their stay it was wall-to-wall beds. If, for any reason, Diego was sent home, usually when Alex and Tyler were at each other, the child cried his eyes out until we promised to fetch him as soon as possible. Somehow, they all survived sharp objects, rusty nails, and their river and arroyo adventures. Into adulthood, the boys all agreed that summer was a magic time.

Accidental Anthropologists

Then trouble began to overtake Diego's life. Over time, the trouble would spill over to us in a number of ways. Pilar told me that it was Perfecto, who started Diego on his life of crime, at the age of two and a half. Perfecto had just been hired as our new postmaster, and one day he locked himself out of the old post office. When he saw a little window open, and Diego approaching him, he grabbed the little boy and hoisted him up to the window. The child was able to jump down inside and open the door for Perfecto. They laughed about that for years. During Perfecto's tenure, village children dropped into the post office on a regular basis for a quick chat with their friend. Our postmaster had a great sense of humor and especially enjoyed the children of San Ignacio.

When Diego and Ines were five, one of them swiped a dozen eggs from home. The two little boys wandered around the village, throwing eggs at windows. They were quickly found out, and the village dealt with it in an interesting manner. Every time Ines and Diego showed up at the post office, Perfecto told them about "the theft" in the village. He would describe in detail all the known facts about the case, even giving the ages of the culprits. Neither Perfecto nor others in the village ever named the vandals. They just continued repeating the story as often as possible, especially when folks were gathered for their daily mail, and the little boys were present.

By the time, he was thirteen, Diego was in enough trouble to wind up in a juvenile correction facility. It didn't take long for him to gain a reputation as a thief. From there, he moved on to breaking and entering people's homes. He even stole a chainsaw from Thomas. We were fortunate to get it back from the man whom Diego tried to sell it to for $25.

Claudia Clavel

The boy just couldn't restrain himself when it came to doing things the wrong way. The first time Thomas and I went to the courthouse in Santa Teresa to see the judge about Diego, the boy was led into the room with shackles on his ankles. Handcuffs bound his hands. I had to stifle a sob. We got him released and became his guardians for a few months, but we couldn't bear it as we watched him sitting on the edge of our little mesa, looking toward home. He did that day after day, until we took him to his Aunt Francesca, where he could be in his own culture and with his cousins.

The three of us had recently watched the movie "The Gods Must Be Crazy," and that was much on our minds as we made the transition: Kalahari Bushmen were known to die if they were locked up for very long, away from their families. We think that made a big impression on Diego, for over the years, he asked to see the movie again and again.

As long as we lived in San Ignacio, we would see that powerful connection between everyone in the village. However, Diego did not die, though he moved from one correctional facility to another for the next several years. Thomas and I visited him at a Boys' Ranch and another time at a boot camp in the southern part of the state. I did not join Thomas in visiting Springer Boys' School, when Diego was interned in that dreadful place. We were good about writing and sending a little money now and then for necessities.

Eventually, he landed in big boy prison, and we started getting disturbing reports about his behavior inside. We had been there for him all along the way, but when we heard during the last two years of his sentence that he had become a prison gang leader and was dealing drugs from the inside, we pulled back from our support.

Accidental Anthropologists

The last straw for us came when we heard that Diego thought of us as "suckers" because we helped him out. By then we had enough experience with some people becoming dependent on us when they needed money, and we knew if we continued being supportive of Diego, we could be solely responsible for him when he got out.

Village neighbors had let us know that we should not let Diego stay with us again, because he had broken into a home and ransacked it before he was jailed the first time. It's a sad truth that played out too often in people's lives. The valley could be harsh on those who refused to play by village rules. We had been told on one occasion that Diego planned to take revenge on all the people who stopped supporting him during his time in prison. We figured his threat probably included us. We tried not to take that too seriously. Prison can often become a place where losing one's grip on reality comes too easily.

When we heard that Diego was about to get out of state prison, we were understandably nervous. He had served eight years for a variety of crimes, including shooting out of the driver's window at a police car that was chasing him. Now 28, Diego had been incarcerated on and off for a long time.

So, when Diego called us right after his release, we shared our concerns with friends, who offered us a safe haven if we felt the need to get away for a while. We thought hard about that, and then decided that Diego was someone we cared about and would have to deal with at one time or another. We decided to stay put. Just then, the phone rang, and it was our young friend, saying he would like to come visit. We said yes.

When Diego showed up at our door early on a Saturday evening, it was the first time we had met in a long time. The Diego who stepped into our kitchen was the grownup version of the boy we had nurtured during his early years, except that he was heavier and more muscular from years of working out. Thomas and I couldn't help but stare, because Diego was tattooed from head to toe. He appeared to be in a hyper-manic phase or on some speedy drug, for he talked a mile a minute, and without a pause he pulled off his shirt and began running his hands over his muscular body, pointing out each tattoo and what it symbolized.

We could see the ex-con had found some of the best prison tattoo artists in the state, for he had his entire family etched into his body. We easily recognized his sister-in-law, Monica, now divorced from Diego's brother, Aaron, and his cousin Eloy, who had hung himself two years after a Marine deployment at the beginning of the Iraq war. Eloy had been part of the group of young boys who integrated themselves into our summer life whether our grandsons were here or not.

Then there was Bobby, Diego's little brother, tattooed on Diego's stomach, his young face captured in ink and frozen in time at age thirteen. Bobby, who had sat at our computer on a Wednesday afternoon working on a Science Fair project, and by nine the next morning, was dead. The boy had been riding in his grandfather's car when they were hit head-on by his uncle. Both men were driving on their way to, and from the school bus stop.

The shock to us had been even more pronounced as we sat in the middle of the church in the big crowd gathered for Bobby's funeral and heard chains rattling at the entrance. Without turning to look, Thomas and I knew in a heartbeat that Diego was being ushered up the aisle. Two sheriff's deputies flanked the young convict, dressed in an orange jumpsuit. His hands were cuffed in front of him, and there were shackles on his ankles. Diego shuffled his way to the casket that sat in front of the altar while his mother screamed uncontrollably, and we sobbed for the grief that continued to plague that family.

So there we were, the three of us standing in our kitchen, trying to take it all in, after so many tragedies and years of confinement. After Diego's tattoo tour, we sat down at our table, where we had shared many meals with him when he was a boy. Just as I started to ask what he would like to drink, Diego asked whether I might have hibiscus tea. He said, "I've been thinking about hibiscus tea for eight years. I can taste it. Oh, I hope you have some."

As it happened, I had made a pitcher that morning. As we sat with Diego and reminisced about his childhood and "messed-up life," as he had always referred to it, he asked, "Would you please invite me to dinner, and serve artichokes with that dip and stuffed peppers with rice? I thought about all the foods you used to serve me when I was little. After all these years, I still remember the tastes." (On reflection, we were pretty sure Diego would never shoot the cook.)

We looked at photographs of Andrew, Tyler and Alex, also now grown up, who had been like brothers to Diego. We reminisced for a while, reliving some of their summer adventures and then sat in silence for a moment, choked up by the thought of innocence lost. As the evening wore on, still talking a mile a minute, Diego gulped down his entire childhood in three tall glasses of hibiscus tea. And then, after hugs, he was off like a shot, just the same as when he was three or four years old, darting out of Thomas's shop with nothing other than a "Bye."

It dawned on me a few days after this visit that Thomas and I were nowhere to be seen on Diego's tattooed body. Even though, over the years he had referred to us as his second parents, there was not one spot of ink that hinted at our relationship. All the tattoo art represented blood relatives. The young man must have endured agonizing pain and bloodletting, from the sheer magnitude of the images. It seemed that Diego had sacrificed himself, through the physical pain of tattoo art, to atone for the pain he had caused his family and to honor them for that.

The culture of northern New Mexico has always been based on bloodlines, and we had never been a part of that. We were of a different culture, and that simply made it impossible to be included in his family. I felt a flood of relief spread over me. Thomas and I decided that Diego had released us from that improbable tie by not including us in his family tree, etched on his body.

We didn't see Diego again and had no word of him until recently, when we were at a gathering where one of his childhood friends happened to be. Gabriel told us that he heard Diego had moved to Denver where his brother Aaron lived. The fact that he left the valley was a positive sign, for we felt that he would never be able to stay out of trouble in his old neighborhood. We figured Diego came to see us to be sure we still cared about him. He cried and begged for our forgiveness, and when he was sure we had done that, it seemed that was all he needed from us. That, and memories he could hold onto forever. We no longer worried about a threat.

9

Gabriel

Gabriel was so thin that when he turned sideways, he almost ceased to exist. We all celebrated when he finally reached one hundred pounds, but that wouldn't happen until he was in his twenties.

In his violent world, the boy was an anomaly. Gabriel didn't smoke or drink, or do drugs. In that environment, the boy was a pure soul, and he was guileless. Without notice, because he was so quiet, Gabriel seemed to slip in between people and then fade into the background.

He came into our life when he was about twelve. He was a couple years older than the other boys who hung out at our house in the summers, but he looked and acted much younger. In his own way, the boy slipped into our lives like a shadow. That was because of Diego, who was his best friend. Diego showed up one summer day with Gabriel in tow, and from then on, the boy was never left out. It was accepted by all that Gabriel belonged to the growing tribe of summer boys.

At that time, there were seven boys: grandsons Alex, Tyler and Andrew, and the local boys: Diego, his brother Aaron, and their cousins Ines and Damian. With Gabriel, the group grew to eight. And they were close, as close as first cousins. In the local Hispanic culture, even fourth cousins were counted. Except for Gabriel, all the boys had spent every summer together from the time they were three and four years old. At least part of every summer day was spent frolicking in the tepid water of the swimming holes. With my bottomless pitchers of hibiscus tea and snacks to go around, we became a place to gather for all the boys. Every year, as summer drew to a close, the group huddled closer and closer together. They never wanted it to end.

Once the boys reached their early teens, the highlight of the season became their trip to the Blue Hole in Santa Rosa, toward the end of summer. Thomas piled all eight of them in the car, along with provisions for a hamburger and hotdog cookout. A watermelon was never left behind. The village river didn't offer much opportunity for real swimming, as most of the activity involved jumping off rocks into one six-foot hole or another. The Blue Hole and little lake in the center of Santa Rosa offered the boys a chance to develop their swimming skills. That is, all but Gabriel, who was terrified of water. When Gabriel was little, his dad had thrown him into the river, where he nearly drowned. He seemed content to watch from the sidelines as his friends hurled themselves off the twenty-five-foot cliff into the eighty-foot-deep Blue Hole.

Jumping off the cliff became a test for all the boys. On those blistering hot afternoons, when a thunderstorm rolled in and lightning drew closer to the Blue Hole, many a timid pubescent boy hurled himself off the cliff, as though being propelled by a lightning bolt. Thomas said a great cheer would go up from the group as each terrified boy finally conquered his fear. To celebrate, they moved to the little lake in the city park, where they feasted on Thomas's grilled burgers and hotdogs and waited for the storm to roll through.

Accidental Anthropologists

The drive to the Blue Hole was a roundtrip of 160 miles, so talk on the way to Santa Rosa was always about who would be the first guy to finally have the courage to make the big leap into the icy water. On the drive home, talk continued over who had found his courage. Not just on the cliff, but in the water as well. Thomas had been a good and patient swim teacher, so by the time the boys all reached adulthood, each of them had become comfortable in the water. They always talked about their experience at the Blue Hole. Except for Gabriel, who had yet to make the leap. The other boys agreed that the experience had been their personal rite of passage into manhood.

During their final trip to the Blue Hole, Aaron and Diego's younger brother, Bobby, was finally old enough to join the ritual. Bobby had just turned thirteen. Thomas told me that the boy spent the entire afternoon sitting on the edge of the high cliff, trying to work up enough nerve to jump. The poor little guy would get up, walk to the jumping-off spot, and then freeze in his tracks, as the other boys called out encouraging words.

As the afternoon wore on, Bobby was on the verge of tears as he saw thunderheads gathering. With one eye on the clouds and one final burst of energy, the boy jumped up, ran to the edge and hurled himself off the cliff. At that very moment, there was a loud thunderclap. Even the lifeguards were cheering just before they called everyone out of the water. Bobby was dancing around, shouting and laughing about how "bad" it had been. He couldn't wait to do it again and again. However, the storm turned out to be big, and the day was fading, so they headed home. Sadly, Bobby would never have another opportunity to jump into the Blue Hole.

Many things changed after that trip: Diego started getting into trouble with the law. Alex went to live with his dad for a few years and missed out on the summer trips.

Claudia Clavel

Ines and Damian's lives changed, too, and we saw Gabriel less frequently, though he and Chonita, his mom, and his little brother, Ambrose, used to stop by to visit now and then. However, once Gabriel entered high school in Santa Teresa, Thomas became a father figure to him, simply due to logistics. The high school was just two blocks from the print shop where Thomas worked. Gabriel started turning up there more and more frequently, as he was plainly skipping school. Thomas would either walk the boy back to school or drive him and wait in the car until he was sure Gabriel was inside. Finally, Thomas sat him down and offered an incentive to finish school. Thomas and I had talked about the problem, and we agreed we would be willing to throw a graduation party for Gabriel if he would finish school.

Gabriel had never had a party in his life. In addition, a graduation party was a very big deal in the valley. As shy as he was, we were a bit surprised at how quickly Gabriel warmed to the idea. We picked the date, and Thomas continued escorting the boy back to school now and then, until graduation day. We sat with Chonita and Ambrose during the ceremony and beamed with pride. Gabriel had made it through. We began making plans for his party.

Just at that time, Demetrio, Chonita's boyfriend and father of Ambrose, was released from prison. He had served three years for drug-related crimes and came to us asking to help with the party. Demetrio had heard we were nice people, and he told us he needed to be around a different crowd. Before prison, the man had been a master stonemason. He asked if we could hire him for a low wage in order to get his skills back up to speed.

We had massive piles of river rock from years of digging holes for various projects. Our dream had always been to build river rock planters around the place. Demetrio was our dream-come-true. We asked if he could work for ten dollars an hour, but he said, "No, but I can work for eight dollars an hour. I told you, I'm probably slow, and you shouldn't have to pay for that."

The next day, he started on a planter next to the summerhouse. That was also the time, when the roof blew off Thomas's shop. We had to scramble to build something to house our freezer and other things left exposed in the roofless ruin. Demetrio came to our rescue, when he salvaged the old roofing lumber and built a little room on the back of the garage. He even brought a glass door that he had made himself a few years back. He said it was a shed-warming gift. We couldn't believe how quickly and cheaply that project came together. Demetrio did a fine job, and we hired him for other projects.

Graduation parties in the area were notorious for getting out of control by the end. We couldn't imagine that happening with Gabriel. We told him to invite whomever he wanted, but he had to let us know how many people were coming. Demetrio said he wanted to grill the hamburgers and hotdogs. We set everything up in the summerhouse and, on the happy day, shook hands with all of Gabriel's friends and relatives as we led them into our backyard. Everyone seemed to be having a great time, and I was chatting with a group of aunties when I noticed a number of young people going back and forth between the backyard and front yard. Then I started hearing chatter about a fight, but I didn't relate it to anything to do with us. People finished eating and said their good-byes, and we began cleaning up.

The phone was ringing as I entered the kitchen, and it was a woman who said she was Gabriel's aunt. She was calling to apologize for calling the police to our party. She said, "I shouldn't have punched Roman, but he had been hitting his girlfriend, who was holding their baby, and I couldn't just stand there." She went on, "Roman was drunk, but that was no excuse."

I nearly fell over. Thomas came in just then, and I nearly shouted, "What has been going on out there? Did you know about this?" Thomas said he thought it best that I didn't know what was happening at the time.

Roman, Gabriel's older brother, had been invited to join the party but chose to stand out front, drinking beer. We had specifically told people there would be no alcohol. The more Roman drank, the more he started picking a fight with his girlfriend. I had never heard of such raw jealousy. However, that wasn't uncommon in his world. The good part was the fact that Gabriel and I were unaware of what was going on in our driveway. I thanked Thomas for sparing us, and we did have a chuckle over the fact that even we Anglos weren't immune to graduation party rumbles.

Demetrio worked for us into summer, finishing the garage addition and his wonderful river rock planter. He capped it with flagstone so I could sit on it while picking vegetables. The next summer, Thomas hired Gabriel to help him tear down his old shop walls. After we had around 1200 adobes made, the young man stacked bricks, side by side, with Thomas until they had the walls up. They were both amazed by what they had accomplished, especially considering that the two of them weighed less than 250 pounds total. Hefting thirty-five-pound adobe bricks all day was no easy task.

When Gabriel was in his twenties, we suffered with him through a number of doomed romances. He looked and acted so young and naïve, he was forever attracting under-age girls and running to us when things fell apart. Thomas, especially, did a lot of counseling for a few years. Eventually, when Gabriel was around thirty years old, he married a Santa Teresa girl named Chita. They had met at a funeral dinner. As Chita told the story, "I looked at Gabriel and thought, boy, is he cute. I'm taking him home with me." And that's just what she did. From then on, they were never apart. Thomas and I loved seeing Gabriel coming through our door with that face: he never stopped smiling. We were especially happy to hear that Chita was twenty-five years old when they met. The couple became Home Health workers, taking care of elderly relatives.

A few months ago, Gabriel called to say he had lost fifteen pounds and was down to eighty-five pounds. They had lost two of their clients to death and hadn't had enough money for food. We packed a big box of provisions, and Thomas hauled it over to their trailer, only to find they didn't have a working refrigerator. They said a cousin would let them use his for storing perishables.

We had a recent visit from Gabriel. He came to tell us that he and Chita had new clients, and they signed up for low-income housing in Santa Teresa. We were happy to hear that news, for we thought life would be a lot easier for them in the little city. There are many elderly people waiting for someone just like Gabriel and Chita to provide loving care. It won't be too long before we'll add our names to that list. It would be another unbroken circle of life in the valley.

10

It Took a Village

The summer our grandson Alex turned fifteen, our quiet life went out the door. Perhaps it had to do with the fact that Thomas was teaching the boy to drive his little Chevy pickup truck. That soon provided Alex a newfound freedom, and the beginning of my summer of torment. As August ambled on toward fall, neighbors began calling to alert us to the driving habits of our grandson. Usually Alex was driving too fast, but one time a neighbor up on the mesa dropped by with a bag of trash Alex was supposed to have taken to the Refuse Transfer Station. Instead, the boy had thrown the bag into a little ditch alongside the back road. It seemed we were always trying to rein in our hyperactive grandson, and we did appreciate everyone's help, even though nothing much made an impact on Alex until his gramps took his driving privilege away.

Alex had a job that summer, working in a little café just a few miles downriver from San Ignacio. To save us the effort of driving Alex to and from work, we allowed him to drive the back dirt road. That is where he had tossed the trash. Having the responsibility of a job did make a difference, and as he began stockpiling money, changes came over him. In some ways, they were good.

Claudia Clavel

In others, they were not so good. Near the end of summer, Alex had become too confident in himself, and he developed a defiant attitude that manifested in more bad driving habits. He was grounded again for a while.

It took a lot to rile my patient better half, but I was beginning to fray at the edges and felt in need of some kind of relief. Then, I remembered a routine we had witnessed in the village on a number of occasions when we were out walking. It was a ritual that went something like this: When things got out of balance in someone's life in the village, they simply drove their car up the hill to the cemetery, turned off the engine, opened the door, turned on the radio and lit a cigarette. They sat in the driver's seat for as long as needed, gazing out at the beautiful scene in front of their windshield. It didn't seem to take long before they had it all figured out, for we could often hear their engine start before we arrived home from our walk.

One particularly hot summer day when I couldn't take it any longer, I got in the car, drove up to the cemetery, opened the door and turned on the radio. I didn't smoke a cigarette. However, I did gaze out the windshield for a while and waited for some feeling of calm that never came. After some time, I drove back down the steep hill but couldn't bring myself to head up our driveway, so I just kept driving very slowly to the plaza.

I drove around the church, and then around again. As I drove, Gilbert rode up on his horse and came alongside me. I didn't stop but just kept driving slower than ever, as he asked if everything was okay. Since everybody in the village knew about Alex, Gilbert didn't have to ask about my strange behavior, he just started counseling me about teenage boys. In addition, he knew what he was talking about, because he had one of his own. We went around a few more times, until Gilbert ran out of advice, and then he headed off toward his place. However, I still wasn't ready to go home so just kept driving in a circle around the church.

The next thing I knew, Palemon pulled up beside me on his four-wheeler. He said, "Claudia, we never see you driving around the village like this. Something must be troubling you." By then, I was on the verge of tears and couldn't tell whether it was over our problem child or the kindness and concern from my neighbors. Palemon rode along with me as we circled the church, time after time. He continued to counsel me from his own experience with his teenage son, Derrick, who by then was a grown man. Round and round we drove, until Palemon apparently had said all he wanted to say on the subject. He turned off at their place, and I headed home slowly, allowing all the advice to soak in. By the time I parked in the garage, I was filled with gratitude for the village ritual that I had just experienced.

When Alex and Tyler were very young, Euservia took care of them while their mother worked at the Santa Teresa hospital for a short while. The little boys loved being dropped off at the Valdez place, for they knew they were in for a series of treats. Euservia perched them on stools so they could watch her make the day's tortillas, and she was generous in allowing them to pinch off pieces of dough to make tiny ones for each other. The three of them had an afternoon ritual of playing cards, and she wouldn't hesitate to take them fishing if they asked. The little boys howled when they had to move away from their dear friend. To the present day, our adult grandsons continue to talk about their boyhood experiences in San Ignacio and the compassion they felt from our neighbors as they were growing up.

11

House Gifts

Over the years, Thomas and I had been on the receiving end of gift giving. Part of it had to do with our resourcefulness in restoring just about anything. We were masters at that craft. Friends brought us pieces of furniture they had tired of, or left-over building materials. We received many calls with offers of all kinds. However, we had never been offered a house before. That was a new one.

Some new friends had recently bought property next to their ranch where the little house was located. It was in a state of near-ruin, with a collapsed roof and water-damaged floors. Local teens had been partying in the house, and the Martins' were concerned about a fire or worse, given how wild the parties had become. One early June day we received a phone call from Walt and Nan, asking whether we would like to have the 1936 Sears Roebuck kit house. He said he had planned to demolish the house, but had heard through mutual friends that I was in need of a studio. He said we would have to move it or take it down. At first, either option seemed like a daunting task, but we were willing to try. In my mind, a free house was nothing to sneeze at and I was desperate for a workspace. We talked to our neighbor Alfredo Rodriguez and asked him to look at the old house, to see whether he thought he could tackle the project. The thing we treasured about people of the valley was the fact that, like us, they were willing to try anything no matter how difficult the job.

We drove Alfredo and Cassandra, with their two toddlers to the Martin ranch and did an inspection of the old structure. Just as we had thought, the couple jumped at the opportunity to dismantle the little house and make some money. Alfredo told us that keeping the demolition crew supplied with Pepsi was part of the deal. Walt told us that the shingles on the sides of the house contained asbestos and had to be removed and disposed of in a special manner. Thomas was able to borrow the equipment needed for the removal and did that job himself.

We still had our big cattle truck so we turned it and a twelve-pack of Pepsi over to Alfredo and Cassandra. They kept Big Truck at the site until the house was taken apart and stacked in the truck. It took a while before we had enough money to put in a foundation, so it was over a year before Alfredo began the task of reassembling the house. The timing couldn't have been better because I was ready to make some art.

The couple had not marked any of the lumber, so it was like putting a puzzle together. They had sorted the wood and had stacks of 2x4's from the interior, along side 12" exterior planks. Another pile was made up of warped maple hardwood flooring and another of ash sub-flooring. The remaining stack was made up of roof framing lumber, I could see Alfredo from my kitchen window as he stood in front of the foundation, obviously deep in thought as he tried to re-imagine the layout. To save him from that problem, I ran out to tell him that it didn't matter how it used to be. I wanted something very different.

The house was 15-by-25 feet, with an upstairs attic loft that had served as a bedroom. There had been two small rooms downstairs. I wanted one big room with the sink at one end and lots of wall space for art shows. It didn't matter where the front door was located, and I knew where the small windows should be placed. I heard a big sigh of relief from Alfredo. He started on the project right after that.

We had a near-crisis just after he got the framed side-walls in place. Alfredo was working on a job in Alamos when a huge wind blew in from the north. It was strong enough to shut down his Alamos job, so he hie-tailed it to our place. I watched in horror as the framed walls were about to topple over, but Alfredo arrived just in the nick of time. The two of us, fueled by an adrenalin rush managed to get the walls upright and stabilized.

The hardwood floors in the little house were badly warped from rain pouring in through the damaged roof. Alfredo spent hours gently tapping the bent wood into the sub-floor, using a rubber mallet. We spent a month sanding floors and hired a Mexican plaster expert to texture the walls and attic ceiling. Finally, it was wired, plumbed and painted, and ready for me to continue creating art. I was able to resume work on my hand-painted clothing line before venturing on to fine art.

A few years after the studio was finished, one of Thomas' co-workers came to visit. Ken, an artist, told Thomas that he, his wife, and three young children had lived in the Sears Roebuck house for eight years, many years before it came to us. Ken sat on the staircase, and as he told his story tears streamed down his cheeks. He said it had been one of the happiest times in his life. He was so happy the house had been given to us, and that it would be used to make art. It was a wonderful house-warming gift.

Not too long after Big Truck had been emptied of the Sears house, we sold the vintage vehicle to a local rock harvester for five hundred dollars and ten cords of firewood. The sale took place in spring, which in the valley was a strange time to have a massive woodpile show up in your yard. Shortly after the delivery, a carload of neighbors drove up to ask us why we had so much wood. We explained that it was a trade for our old truck, and that seemed to satisfy them. In the early years, people

Claudia Clavel

were always fishing to find out whether we might have money. Trust-fund hippies had a bad reputation left over from the '70s, and locals weren't shy about asking those questions.

The first show in my new studio featured my pen-and-ink drawings depicting the surrounding landscapes. For a number of years on a biweekly basis, I shared my creative space with four women artist friends when we gathered to make art and eat a potluck lunch together. On one of those days, our friend, Blair brought a big bag filled with painted paper from a workshop she had attended at Ghost Ranch. The paper was torn into pieces and used in creating *collàge* landscapes. I was hooked on that from the beginning and worked on acrylic ink-stained paper *collàge* for around five years.

After a number of shows, I began to lose interest in *collàge* and produced less and less. Over the years, my creative interests usually ran a course and then I moved on to something new. However, it was always a bit of a shock when I knew it had ended, especially when I was selling well and loved the process. It took some time to realize that New Mexico had started to dry out, and we began to hear the word drought. The beautiful flora surrounding us had slowly begun to disappear, including the hardy high-desert wildflowers. It was then that I realized how much color had been my inspiration. As the landscape turned into patches of dried buffalo grass clinging to parched red earth, my creative interests turned to other ventures. Up to that point, I had visually chronicled the changing seasons during our time in the village. I had no desire to interpret the drying out of the state.

From then on, my interests moved to building projects. We had started with one old adobe house, Thomas's funky workshop, and an outdoor shower. Perfecto had been impressed by the gift of the old Sears Roebuck kit house, and one day asked if we would like to have another house. I asked what he had in mind, and he told me that he and Pilar wanted to get rid of her grandma's old adobe house, which sat right next to their home. The house was blocking the sun from their south wall in winter, and they wanted more open space.

Perfecto said we would have to take the house down, but we could have all the adobes, windows and doors. He offered us the fourteen *vigas* for a very fair price. In essence, it was a complete house. I told him I would talk to Thomas about it and let him know the next day. Perfecto said, "Well, you have to hurry a bit because I have a friend with a backhoe and time to get it leveled." There was nothing like a deadline to push us into action.

Thomas agreed to the offer, and soon the two of us started on the project. We somehow got the roof off, and then Thomas began to tap the big adobe bricks with a rubber mallet. They were held together with adobe mud mortar, and it was fairly easy to break them loose. As he loosened a brick, he handed it to me and I stacked them into piles.

An adobe brick weighs thirty-five pounds. At that time, I was fifty-five years old and weighed 125 pounds. What neither of us had considered was the fact that the bricks had to be stacked three times; once on the ground, the second time on a flatbed trailer loaned to us by Perfecto. On the third time, the bricks were unloaded and restacked at our place.

As we were busy dismantling the house, neighbor men drove by and stopped to watch and call out encouraging words. Women in San Ignacio did not do heavy outdoor work, so I became something out of the ordinary, especially at my age. As a result, it became a bit of a spectator sport for our neighbors. By the time, Thomas and I finished the demolition project; we both agreed that we would never accept another gift house.

One of the first things Thomas created at our place was the outdoor shower. A tub bath in the heat of summer was not the best option, especially with lots of visitors.

We had plenty of privacy, so Thomas created a space behind his shop for the shower. He built a fence around two sides and fastened a water line to the inside of one of them

Claudia Clavel

. The line was connected to the water heater in the little laundry room, so there was always soft-as-silk hot water. The shower faced the mesa and arroyos below, so the view from that spot was stunning. Evening showers became the highlight of our days, especially when coyotes were howling their heads off as a full moon came up. We showered out there for over twenty years, turning it into a game as we dared ourselves to shower into colder and colder weather. When it began to freeze at night we moved indoors for winter baths.

Our daughter, Cyndi and her significant other, Larry came every summer for a few years to help with building projects. Larry was a very creative woodworker, and Cyndi became his assistant. Between the two of them, they added many great features to our building projects. At the end of their annual two-week stay, Larry always presented us with a surprise hand-made gift that he had created, using old weathered wood from our huge pile.

One year Larry made a little cabinet with a glass front door for the outdoor shower. We had been losing bars of soap to pack-rats or squirrels, so the gift was much appreciated. The following year he fashioned a shaving stand with a mirror that we hung on the shower fence. The most creative gift was a replica of my studio, about 3 feet long, with the wrap-around glass porch. Larry had cut out little windows and framed them. Then he topped it all off with a copper roof.

Cyndi and Larry worked every summer evening during their stay until, eventually they finished a beautiful low, stacked stonewall next to the studio. They placed flat stones on top so we could sit on the wall and watch sunsets.

We used all the old adobe bricks in constructing a summerhouse on the north side of our main house. We had plenty of windows for the project. Thomas used large ones, set in three walls, and built the south wall entirely of windows, including the doors. Our neighbor Lorenzo Casados had given us enough old log *vigas* for the roof support, and he recruited a couple of

Accidental Anthropologists

friends to help set them in place. Because she thought it was a perfect fit, Blair sold us her little wood cook stove for a pittance.

Old friends, who were world travelers, gave us enough hand-woven Indonesian fabric to make *banco* (bench) covers and a dozen pillows. Douglas, our potter friend, was so taken by the charm of the room that he made us a set of dishes using the Indonesian fabric designs and colors on the surface of the plates and saucers. I hung, an 18-cup candelabra over the table and transformed the space into a flickering light show as the evening light faded. The little building became a source of delight for all the people in our life. For many years, we entertained there with endless summer dinner parties and, especially tea parties.

Thomas laid a flagstone patio in front of the summer-house. A co-worker gave us his old Franklin fireplace, and Thomas set it up on the edge of the patio, with a chimney pipe reaching skyward. Not long afterward, he called from work to tell me he had just purchased four patio chairs and a short table at the Salvation Army store. He said they were all made out of rubber tires and were painted green. I could not imagine such a bizarre sight, but was won over when he brought them home. The chairs were incredibly comfortable and quite the conversation pieces. Our friends and grandsons loved sitting in those chairs, toasting marshmallows in the old Franklin stove. We were being hooked on creative building projects. It was a good thing too, as we were soon faced with a disaster that would test our skills.

A number of years after Thomas donated his silkscreen shop's equipment to a Boys' Detention School a ninety-mile-per-hour wind gust blew the roof off the old shop.

We had Montana guests who were sleeping in their camper when they were shaken awake. It was in April at midnight, with a full moon, as Jerry watched half the roof fly two stories over the house and onto the road below. He didn't wake us. He decided there was nothing we could do at that point. When Thomas awoke and went to brush his teeth, his gaze was pulled to a window in the bathroom. The other half of the

81

peaked roof, covered with sheet metal, had fallen down into the yard, where it was rocking back and forth toward the house. It was a very scary sight, and in the high wind, a dangerous thing to deal with.

A neighbor came running to our rescue with a big rope and a spike. He pounded the spike into the ground and then jumped on the rocking roof. The man studied the situation and determined where to attach the rope in order to create enough tension to keep it from moving.

It turned out there was a wedding that day in the village, and the half of the roof that had blown into the road had cut a power line. A repairperson made it in time for the event, but the poor wedding party had been greatly inconvenienced. Our neighbors were more than understanding, especially as they realized what we had to deal with that day.

Once the part of the roof in our yard was secure, we took Jerry and Cathy for a hike at the Tent Rocks and stopped at Bert's Burgers on the way home for green chile burgers. We needed time to reflect on our latest disaster.

It took a few years, but we eventually pulled the old shop back together and turned it into a luxurious casita. Once that was finished, we added a sun porch for solar gain. I had become the building superintendent and soon learned to love the process. It became great fun for me to figure out how many boards and how much sheetrock we would need. I spent days on the phone getting prices and running back and forth to lumber yards with endless lists of building supplies.

For many years, we went from one building project to the other. We added a garage and then a little room attached to the garage to house a freezer and extra fridge. The shed, as we called it, was constructed entirely from the old shop roof. From then on, we began calling our place Casa Debris.

When I was a child, my maternal grandmother built her own hotel in Kansas and later a triplex. I remember seeing her at age eighty-five, snow-white hair, dressed in a pair of overalls,

Accidental Anthropologists

sitting on the street curb with a hammer in one hand and a nail in the other. She was pounding the crooked nail straight so the carpenter could use it on a recycled board for a wall. It dawned on me that I came by the trade naturally. It was obviously in my genes.

12

Macario

The first time we encountered Macario, he was lying face down on the cattle guard where we turned off the paved road onto the dirt road into the village. It was midnight, and thank God, somebody was behind us who knew Macario and his habits. The driver signaled us to go ahead, and looking back, we saw someone get out of the car and bend over his passed-out body. Our next encounter with Macario occurred a few weeks later, when he arrived at our door, "three sheets to the wind," as my father would have said. He had been on the road below our house, directing friends of ours who were trying to find our house. Macario could spot a party a mile away and assumed we would invite him in. By then, we knew better.

Shortly after we turned Macario away, we became aware that we no longer had water. During that particular time, this occurred frequently. Constant water flow depended on who the *pumpero* was at the time, for the big standing storage tank had to be monitored. This did, however, shut our party down early since beer was the drink of the day, and the toilet had been in full use.

By the third waterless day, we began asking neighbors their water status and learned we were the only ones with a problem. Hearing that news, Thomas slapped his forehead and headed down to the main water valve. Sure enough, it had been turned off. I heard Thomas shout "Bastard!" and I knew it was Macario who had shut it off the day he was refused entrance to our party.

One brilliant sunny day, a friend came to visit, and as we walked out to her car, we heard and then saw Macario below us on the plaza, surrounded by his faithful dogs. Lizzie had seen Macario the day of our party, so she knew a bit of the man's history. On numerous occasions, I had seen him in the plaza, shouting and throwing rocks at village boys. Just then, the old man began reeling around, his arms flailing.

Suddenly, Macario began to shout obscenities, as he kicked up a large cloud of dust that enveloped him and his dogs. Lizzie asked whether the old man was dangerous, and I replied, "Only if he has a gun." At that very moment, the guy pulled out a gun and began shooting into the air. His dogs were barking and swirling around him. We ran into the house as Lizzie shouted, "Jeezus, how can you guys live like this?" It wasn't the first time someone had asked us that question. And we did ask it ourselves at times.

A few days later at the post office, a neighbor and I were talking about Macario and whether he might be seriously dangerous to others. He told me that Macario suffered a form of Tourette's syndrome and it was made worse by his drinking. We laughed about some of his antics and then got serious about his use of a gun under the influence. The neighbor had witnessed many years of Macario's behavior. He thought for a while and then asked whether I had ever seen Macario with his chainsaw in action. I replied with some sense of horror that I had not. He went on to tell me about a number of incidents when Macario would get rip-roaring drunk, fire up his chainsaw and careen out into the plaza, challenging man and beast. Needless to say, during those occasions, village residents remained securely behind their doors.

Nonetheless, life in a small village made it impossible to avoid unpleasant people. We had to walk across the plaza to the post office every day. The Drinkers spent at least part of their time in that vicinity, so Macario simply could not be dismissed. Thomas met him formally before I did. When they shook hands, Thomas said Macario would not let go, and he kept squeezing his hand as hard as he could. Thomas went on to say the man's grip was amazing, and it hurt, but he wasn't about to let go. What Macario didn't know, was that Thomas' hands were even stronger, from working in a lumber mill for a few years, where he handled heavy, wet boards. Thomas said the handshake felt like it went on forever. They both kept squeezing, until Macario finally gave in and let go. We learned early on to stand up to people. Any sign of weakness could make your life harder in the long run.

When we met Macario, he was in his sixties. He was a small thin man with a scraggly, gray beard and a big, droopy mustache. He always wore a soiled suit and a stocking cap, summer or winter. Macario was toothless and slurred all his words, drunk or sober, Spanish or English. Hardly anyone understood him-except for me. I had some uncanny ability to decipher whatever came out of his mouth. Because Macario hung out at the post office for a good part of each day, it was inevitable that we would become better acquainted. As he came to realize that I understood him, Macario began behaving differently toward me.

That fall when I began giving flower seeds that I harvested to the women of the village, I asked Macario if

Claudia Clavel

he would like to have some. Whenever we met, the two of us had talked about plants, and he seemed genuinely pleased by my offer. Not long after that, he came to me with a bucket of rose cuttings. I gratefully accepted, for as an artist I was always trying to add color to our barren place.

One exceptionally wet year, word of my bountiful flower gardens reached Macario, and he came up to see for himself. It had been a good monsoon season, so there were cosmos everywhere, and zinnias, baby's breath, Shasta daisies, sunflowers, sweet peas and sweet Williams. Macario walked slowly around the yard, pausing before each plant, and then he gave me the names of all the flowers—in Italian! He was delighted by my surprise and told me he had been stationed in northern Italy at the end of the Second World War. It was there he had picked up the language.

I realized then just how intelligent a character he was and, from that time on, Macario and I developed a friendship. When he was sober, we shared the love of plants and language. When the man was drunk, he never came near me, except for one time in the post office, when he was on a bender. The old man impulsively kissed my hand in front of several neighbors. He looked around, and with a foolish grin, sauntered out the door. I was told Macario had a nickname for me: "*Flacita*." That is Spanish for "dear skinny one."

One cold winter day, I could see my breath as I came out of my studio after lunch. I looked across the plaza, and my heart began to race as I saw smoke and flames at the back of Palemon and Delfinia Archuleta's house. The volunteer fire chief was on their roof with a hose, and people were running in and out of the house, carrying furniture. I ran across the plaza to where Delfinia stood in hysterics. She kept crying repeatedly, "He always said he would do it. For twenty years he's been threatening to burn our house down." She was, of course, talking about Macario. Except in this case, it was his house that was on fire. One of Macario's walls was attached to the Archuleta house, and the fire had spread to their roof. The chief got the roof fire under control, but by then, Macario's house had burned to the ground, taking with it a new litter of puppies. The old man nearly burned to death trying to save the pups. It was said, on good authority, that Macario had thrown a can of kerosene into his wood cook stove to get a fire started. It had exploded in his face, and his hair, eyebrows and beard were severely singed. No one could believe that Macario walked out of that inferno.

The village was so upset with the old man that not one person would offer him a haven. Someone phoned the State Police, and they took him off to Santa Teresa and the police station. Macario spent a few nights in a cell, where he was at least warm and fed. It was March, very cold and snowy, and we all hoped the police would keep him for a while. I was grief stricken—for Palemon, Delfinia and Macario. What would become of the social misfit? The police brought him back to San Ignacio, and he was sober, in more ways than he probably realized. He now had no place to live.

As I was stewing about Macario's wellbeing, other people had already taken action. Immediately after his return, a small travel trailer appeared on his little plot of land. It was placed well away from Palemon and Delfinia's house. Men of the village began building a small, one-room adobe structure next to the trailer. Neighbors came up with everything Macario needed to take up life as usual. We could hardly believe our eyes. All this activity happened within a week or so after the fire.

Claudia Clavel

Neighbors helping neighbor's, remains one of the true wonders of life in rural America.

A day or so after the fire, I took Delfinia and Palemon a homemade coffee cake. I offered to help with her clean-up chores. There was smoke damage, so Delfinia needed to wash all the walls and ceilings. She would have to paint the entire inside of their house.

My neighbor was philosophical about the disaster, and I had to smile at her resolve. She told me that she had been living with the fear of fire for over twenty years. She and Palemon had been at war with Macario all that time. The man had indeed threatened to burn them out when they were first married and moved into Delfinia's grandma's house. Delfinia, had already come to the conclusion that she alone needed to clean and repaint her home. She said it would help her calm her nerves and get her over the shock of their near-tragedy. I reminded her that she and Palemon could now let go of the threat.

A few days after my visit with Delfinia, I drove to the post office on my way to pick up the daily paper at La Tienda. Macario waved me down, looking wilder than ever with his singed eyebrows, hair and beard. He asked for a ride to the Rainbow Club, about a mile and a half up the frontage road. Many of the valley men met there for a beer and gossip. There were a couple of gas pumps, so people were always stopping by. A number of gas pump/bars were sprinkled throughout the valley, and they all served as gathering spots for locals.

As we drove along, Macario looked at me for a while and then asked if I knew about the fire. I replied that I did. After a long pause, he said, "I didn't do it." It was difficult not to laugh, with him sitting there singed beyond belief. However, I realized how important it was for him to have me believe him. I had to choke back tears as he told me about trying to save his puppies.

Accidental Anthropologists

I pulled into the Rainbow Club parking lot as Macario finished his story. He asked if I would wait for him a bit. I was always in a hurry but managed to control my impatience as he headed toward the bar. I thought, "I'll give him five minutes, that's it." It wasn't long before Macario climbed back in beside me. He wore his big, toothless grin, and as he looked at me he said, "I told them you're my girlfriend."

Life went on, and Macario grew old despite his lifestyle. I thought about that a lot, for he wasn't the only one. Then I realized longevity in the village had to do with a feeling of belonging to the community. Every person was accepted on some level, no matter how bad the behavior. Even we, the Anglo outsiders, felt the connection, for it was a village thing. It was a very strong bond.

13

Village Pumpero

Not long after our arrival, Salvador Ortega approached Thomas and asked him to serve as the village *pumpero*. All the small villages in New Mexico had community well water systems that were installed in the 1940s as part of the federal WPA jobs program. The *pumpero* was responsible for maintaining the system day to day.

There was a huge water tank up on the mesa above San Ignacio, where water was stored after being pumped from the well in the plaza. The pump had a timer that was set for high-water usage times: mornings when people were showering and doing laundry and evenings around suppertime. The schedule was determined by whoever was *pumpero* at the time. Sometimes, after a few too many beers, the operator forgot to tend to his business. As a result, the tank wasn't filled, so the village would be without water for hours, until the *pumpero* got back to his job. That pattern had gone on for many years.

Salvador and other men in the village knew Thomas was running a business at home, so they evidently felt he would be a good choice for *pumpero*. Because we were sick and tired of the water outages, Thomas readily agreed to take on the task. What our neighbors couldn't have known at the time was how hyper-focused my spouse was on every front. Right away, he got into the pump timing mechanism and tinkered with it until he had it running smoothly.

Every evening, we walked up the hill to the tank, where Thomas ran his hand up and down the side of the water container. He could feel the water level by the change in temperature on the metal side of the tank. That way, he knew exactly how much water had been used and how to set the timer. Over time, Thomas figured out the rhythms of water use for the whole village. Because of that, he endeared himself to all the women, for we were never again caught waterless in the middle of washing dishes or doing laundry.

Five years later, when Thomas took the town job, a new water system was being installed and there was no longer a need for a *pumpero*. The new water association would require a trained water system operator. He would read monthly home water meters and monitor the fire hydrants and storage tanks. Through federal loans and grants, all the village water systems were being upgraded. Most of the old pipes were leaking more water than people were using, so the change came just in time.

However, it had not been an easy transition. Lorenzo Sanchez and Salvador Ortega had done all the preliminary work to acquire the grants, and next they had to talk everyone in the village into signing on for the loan required to install it. We had paid two dollars a month for unlimited water when we moved in years earlier, and that was up to six dollars by the time the new system was being introduced. Our new rate would be thirty-two dollars a month.

People were outraged by the cost increase, but most eventually signed on. One of the selling points: new fire hydrants that would lower our fire insurance premiums

Accidental Anthropologists

and provide water for the volunteer fire department tanker truck. Until then, the truck had to be filled up at the river before it could be used to fight a fire. Each house in the village had a new water meter installed, with an allotment of 7,500 gallons a month. Going over that amount resulted in higher rates, and that didn't set well with a lot of folks who thought water came from God. They believed no one should have to pay for a God-given utility. The water wars started then.

After his term as *pumpero* ended, Thomas served on the community water board for years in one capacity or another. There was a time at the beginning of the new system when a disgruntled neighbor threatened all the water board members. Shivers went down my spine when Thomas told me, but soon after, the neighbor drove up to tell Thomas he wasn't included in the threat. The man said it had to do with old feuds between him and his neighbors. We didn't know whether to laugh or cry over that one.

When Thomas went to the next water board meeting, he told the other members he thought he should resign, because it didn't seem fair that he was the only one not included in the threat. Demetrio, the board president, then in his late seventies, pulled up his shirt and pointed to a scar as he said, "We've been dealing with threats our entire lives. And we have the scars to prove it. We know how to deal with guys like him. Don't you worry." Thomas responded, "That's what I'm afraid of."

We soon found ourselves in the middle of family feuds and ages-old conflicts, but were always assured by our neighbors that we were not part of it. We were separate in that respect because we had no history in the village. The board members gathered around Thomas, patting him on the back and assured him that things

Claudia Clavel

would work out just fine. As one board member pointed out, "Some people open their mouths, and nothing comes out but wind." And they were right—the threat never materialized.

The problems with the new system began when some people became delinquent in paying their bills. It was up to the water system operator to turn people's water off when they had not paid their bills after three months. Notices were sent out and then registered letters, but for some folks nothing seemed to work. Meetings were held, endless discussions took place, but people didn't pay. In a small village, shutting off a neighbor's water could be seen as an act of terrorism, so no one wanted to be the enforcer.

People began to complain about those who were not paying their fair share, especially if they saw one of them carrying a 30-pack of beer out of La Cantina. On and on it went, with all sides feeling squeezed by injustice. At one point, when a habitually delinquent water user received his umpteenth shut-off notice, he called Thomas, who was the water board treasurer at the time. Alfonso screamed and swore threats to the point that my husband was visibly shaken. For some unknown reason, Alfonso had never liked Thomas, and he made a point of letting everyone know it. To us, he was one scary guy. Once I had seen him shooting a gun on the back road. A bullet ricocheted off a rock wall and hit a tree alongside our driveway, just as our daughter was walking by. She heard the bullet hit the tree, and we found it on the ground below.

It was a couple years after the tree shooting that Alfonso went off on Thomas. As a result, Thomas wrote a letter of resignation to the water board that ended with this statement: "I'm now an old man, and I don't want to have to meet some guy at high noon in the plaza over water." After I read his letter, I thought it sounded pathetic and I urged him not to send it. It was important not to come across as weak in any situation. Thomas had to agree, so he didn't send the letter.

The very next morning, our phone rang. It was Cordero, another water board member, calling to say Alfonso wanted to meet Thomas the next day—at noon—in the plaza. I was in the room and saw my husband's eyes grow wider and wider. I heard him stammer, "Noon! Noon! How about one?" As he put the phone down and told me about the conversation, he said, "I wanted to give myself one more hour." We stood looking at one another in total disbelief. Then we started to laugh. We laughed until we were nearly hysterical. It was right out of a Spaghetti Western and so typical of the place.

Cordero called back right away to say that Alfonso couldn't make it at one. Could Thomas meet them at eight the next morning? Alfonso had insisted Cordero accompany him, and we figured it was to keep him from doing violence to Thomas. As my spouse headed out the door the next morning, he turned to me and said, "Well, at least we'll get it over with sooner." I wished him well as a big knot tightened my throat.

Fortunately, for me, Thomas wasn't gone too long and when he returned, he wore a big grin. I watched him come up the driveway with a piece of paper in one hand. As he entered the kitchen, he waved the paper, which turned out to be a money order. Alfonso had paid all the money he owed. Thomas told me it had been an intense meeting, and the look on Alfonso's face made it clear he still hated the water board treasurer. But never mind, the guy paid his debt.

14

The Lovato Brothers

Not everyone in San Ignacio was Catholic, or even religious. Peter and Joseph Lovato had been given saints' names, probably due to the influence of their mother. However, it wasn't long before their father nicknamed the little boys Pee'te and Joe. The family had no religious interests. They had all lived in Santa Fe for many years before buying property in San Ignacio. The village was a place they had all fallen in love with over the years. Pee'te and Joe were adults by the time the entire family relocated.

The brothers' parents built a house across the road from where each brother had a house with a car repair shop. The Lovato brothers had worked as foreign auto mechanics in the city, and they could hardly wait to set themselves up in their new auto repair business. That simple act set them apart, because their businesses were seen as an infringement on other valley repair shops.

It took several years for us to hear about their business because no one ever mentioned them. That's the way it worked in the area. It was the notorious Victoria, who turned us on to the brothers, because she was driving a foreign car and because she knew all the men in the village. Our car situation in those days was such that we were often in need of a mechanic. At that time, we had a special relationship with the Santa Teresa tow-truck driver. Pee'te became a lifesaver for us, and when he retired to become the village water system operator, we moved on to his brother, Joe.

Now, there was a mechanic! Joe was short and stocky, with a huge grin planted permanently on his face. In addition, he was about the friendliest guy you would ever meet. He seemed to light up as soon as you approached him. As we grew to know him, Joe wouldn't let us take a trip until he had gone over our car from top to bottom. And he wouldn't take money for his efforts. He said he wouldn't be able to live with himself if anything happened to us while we were on the road. We were not getting special treatment; that was the way he treated all his customers.

Joe even had a towing system on his truck and charged a flat fee of twenty-five dollars per tow. If we needed a repair job, the mechanic would insist on walking up to our place to pick up the car, and Thomas had to argue with him about picking it up once it was fixed. The man admittedly lived and breathed to help people.

Joe liked nothing better than to sit around after work with Pee'te, his customers and friends to share a few beers. When Thomas went to pick up our car, he knew he would be a while, because there would be a little party. The brothers were great conversationalists, each with a wry sense of humor, so they always had a group around them.

When Marta moved in with Joe, he felt his life had become complete. They were perfect for one another and very industrious together. The two of them created a lovely covered patio and gardens along the *acequia* ditch behind their house. They loved entertaining in their new space, and it became a great gathering place. When Thomas and I walked past the couple's home in the evenings on the way to the river, we could feel joy spilling out of all their doors and windows. However, as we had seen so often in the village, one moment there could be immense happiness, and in the next, the most profound tragedy. At the height of Joe's new career as a business owner and his luck in love, he was killed in a freak accident.

One scorching summer day, Joe was on horseback with a group of village men. They had been on a weekend camping trip and were on their way home when his horse slipped on a steep trail. Joe was thrown off, and the horse fell on top of him. He died the same week that Eloy took his life and another young man died in a nearby village. The level of grief in the valley was unbearable for a long time. It seemed like the village began growing quieter around that time. We knew for certain, that Joe and Pee'te's end of the village never recovered from the loss.

Pee'te was a slightly built man with a small frame and quite a bushy beard. The man was never still, constantly on the move with one project or another. He and his family always grew a sizeable vegetable garden. They had a small orchard and raised a pig to butcher. Pee'te's wife, Monica, worked full time but found time to can and preserve their bountiful harvests. She was known as a great and creative cook. The couple had two children: a daughter named Maya and a son they called Aaron. We enjoyed their children and hired them over the years to help with simple chores. Children in the village were always seeking ways to earn a few dollars, and we were happy to have their help now and then. Over the years, we tried to spread our little summer jobs around to all the village children.

Pee'te took his job as water system operator seriously, and the village was better off because of his efforts. He never tired of checking water lines for leaks or making endless repairs on little things connected to the system. It was his job to read the water meters on the first of the month, and he had to keep the water hydrants flushed out every now and then. Overall, Pee'te did an awful lot for the village despite the very low pay. Even ill health wouldn't stop the guy from doing his job. To all of us, it appeared the man was a glorified *pumpero,* who kept our water flowing smoothly.

Everyone in the village worried about who would take care of our water system once the elders passed on. Many young people had moved away, and the only ones remotely interested in the water system happened to be Maya and Aaron. After Maya graduated from college, Thomas jumped on that connection and hired her to do the billing and mailing of water bills. Because Aaron had stuck close to home, Thomas talked Pee'te into grooming Aaron as the next system operator, and he did just that. Aaron took the required course, passed the difficult exam and was qualified. There were many reasons for keeping San Ignacio's water system in the village, and everyone agreed that we were lucky to have Pee'te and his family taking care of a precious commodity.

There were other parts to the waterman: He read Shakespeare and once brought me his tattered little 1917 volume of Shakespeare's sonnets because he wanted me to read them. He told me he had circled number twenty-one for my attention.

Pee'te was a Renaissance man who had great affection for art and artists. He was also very creative and could often be seen stacking rocks into creative sculptures or planting flowers in lovely patterns around his place. Like the rest of us in the village, Pee'te was especially adept at creating out of the raw materials that lay all around him.

15

The Funeral

Lazaro and Celina Flores were neighbors who lived on the back road, near the bottom of our driveway. The first time I stepped inside their back door, I knew from the gloomy atmosphere what poverty felt like. A bare light bulb hung from an electric cord in the middle of the room that served as their kitchen. Everything looked to be the same color: a bare earth tone with a dirty cast to it. The raw adobe walls were a dark brown color, not the rosy red so commonly found in that part of the country. An old wood plank floor, turned nearly black from years of wood smoke and infre quent cleaning, seemed to pull you down lower than you wanted to be.

The room held little in the way of furniture: a wood kitchen table with a few chairs strewn around. One sat in front of the wood cook stove, which was still warm from the morning cooking. There were some wood planks on sawhorses along one wall, serving as a counter. The room was huge, which only made the few furnishings seem more insignificant. You didn't want to stay long in that kitchen. It felt menacing and grimy. Not totally hopeless, just rank and oppressive.

And yet, there they sat: the occupants, as grimy and menacing in their own way as their surroundings, bidding me, "Come in, come in and stay awhile" with all the joy they could muster for a friend. The contrast nearly sent me reeling, because I had never been to Lazaro and Celina's home before. The women in the valley were known for their immaculate housekeeping, in spite of the way the villages appeared on the exterior, especially through the eyes of outsiders. I guess I just took for granted that my neighbors' home would be the same as those around them. It never occurred to me that Celina's personal hygiene would mirror that of her dwelling on such an extreme level.

I will attempt to describe Celina, who lived her life on the edge of squalor. She was a large woman, tall for a Hispanic, and heavy breasted. She had huge gnarled feet that were always bare, even in winter. The woman wore nothing but rubber thongs, and her feet were filthy. It was a mystery to me how Celina was able to walk through snow with nothing but rubber soles beneath her feet. Day after day, she wore the same faded house dress, braless and ill fitting.

Celina's hair was a mass of tangles, which she pushed up on the sides of her head. Every now and then, as though by habit, she removed a comb and then shoved it back into the mess. Most often, there would be hair sticking out all around her face. She reeked of wood and cigarette smoke and seemed always to have a cigarette in hand or dangling out of one side of her mouth on her walks up to use our phone. Celina was, literally, one big unkempt mess of a woman. But she had a heart of gold amid all that disarray.

Lazaro and Celina didn't have a telephone and had never had one. That was one necessity they simply could not afford. For a number of years, while they lived in San Ignacio, they used our phone for emergencies and to make a few appointments with doctors and such. We kept a log of their calls, and on the first of every month, Celina came up to pay their bill. They never abused the use of the telephone and always paid their bill on time. It was never a very big inconvenience, and Celina respected my reclusiveness, rarely lingering for conversation. I especially appreciated that consideration. Occasionally, Lazaro would drive his wife up, waiting for her in the pickup truck. On those occasions, I would go out for a chat with him while Celina made her calls.

Lazaro was in his early sixties, a small, spare man with thick, gray hair and a long, kind of wild, beard. His dark eyes were heavy lidded and piercing, until he recognized you. Then they lit up a bit as he began to speak. Lazaro was a serious and chronic alcoholic. I had seen him drunk a number of times throughout the years. He would be shouting and reeling madly out onto the road behind their house. In that state, Lazaro was a mean and vicious threat. I had the good fortune to stay out of his way during those bouts. Otherwise, Lazaro was basically a good person. He was kind and helpful to his friends and family. The man had a great sense of humor and we shared some good laughs. We also shared an interest in gardening and landscaping, so always had things to talk about.

One early morning at the beginning of June, Celina knocked on my back door. She had been crying and was holding a piece of paper in her hand. When I opened the door, Celina stepped inside and put her arms around me. It was so unexpected, I knew immediately something was terribly wrong. She began crying again and it took a little while before she could speak. She released her arms and stepped back a bit, pulling herself together. Finally, she spoke: "Javiel is dead. They murdered him."

Claudia Clavel

I choked back a sob. "Wait a minute," I said. "Tell me what happened."

Javiel was Lazaro and Celina's son, in his late twenties. He worked at a nursing home in Santa Teresa as an aide. He was gay. Now he was dead. He had been murdered! We both sat down at the kitchen table, and Celina told me the story of her son's murder. Javiel lived in one of the low-income housing projects in Santa Teresa, an especially dangerous one to be sure. Two guys who lived in the same project, had been harassing him for some time. According to Celina, "Those two low-life's were always yelling obscenities at Javiel, especially 'fag' and 'queer'."

The murder occurred after those two had been drinking all day. They broke into Javiel's apartment and waited for him to come home from work at midnight. They didn't just murder him; they tortured him for a while with a knife, finally stabbing him to death. I felt faint as Celina told everything she had learned from the police. The State Police knew where to find the Flores. In such a small community, when they couldn't reach them by phone, they simply sent a car out to give the family the news personally.

The piece of paper Celina had been clutching held the phone number of the Red Cross. She was going through them, hoping they would be able to help her get another son home for his brother's funeral. That son, Cosme, was an inmate at Leavenworth Federal Penitentiary in Kansas. I almost laughed with comic relief, after all I had just heard. Celina was almost positive Cosme would be allowed to come home, even though it would require a marshal to accompany him. It seemed reasonable to me, but then I was hoping for something positive to happen for those people.

Accidental Anthropologists

Javiel's funeral was postponed a few days in hopes that Cosme would somehow be allowed home. Days of Red Cross calls brought no response from Leavenworth. Meanwhile, Celina had called her family together from around the country. With each call, I got a little background rundown on a daughter or son. It wasn't very encouraging; all the kids seemed to be having a rough time trying to cope with life. It made me sad and at the same time amazed at how we each have to deal with the hand fate deals us. That family had to find strength to deal with the horror that had just befallen them, just like everybody else in the world. Word finally came that Cosme would not be allowed home for the funeral. By then, I breathed a sigh of relief, for I knew that it would probably have been my fate to be seated next to the marshal and Cosme in shackles.

The day before the funeral, Celina came up to call a florist. I heard her ask the price of a funeral wreath for the casket. "Sixty- five dollars, sixty-five dollars, I don't have that kind of money," she nearly shouted into the receiver. She began to cry, and it was only the second time I had seen her break down since the news of Javiel's death. Suddenly, she blurted out, "Claudia, you have to help me, I can't bury that boy without flowers. It just isn't right."

I sure couldn't help her with money. During that time, there was never an extra cent in our life. "It's the wrong time of year for my flowers," I said. "They won't be blooming for another month." Celina couldn't stop crying. I thought for a moment and then said, "Wait, I saw a rosebush full of red roses at the house on top of the frontage road hill yesterday when I drove by. We could ask those people for their roses." Celina sniffed back the tears as she mumbled, "Nobody lives there, they just moved out."

We looked at one another, and I smiled. "I do have baby's breath in bloom," I said, feeling relief settle over me. Then I went on, "I have a big, old-fashioned basket with a handle. Actually, it looks like a funeral casket flower basket. If your daughters will go up to that house early in the morning and cut the roses, I'll have everything ready to put together a bouquet." Celina dried her eyes, and gave a big sigh of relief. We hugged and both of us felt a lot better.

Seven o'clock the next morning, there was a knock on my back door, and through the window I saw three young women, each holding a big can filled with Red Blaze roses. I opened the door, and the women stepped shyly into my kitchen and introduced themselves.

We set to work immediately. My basket was low and wide, so I was able to set small tin cans full of water all over the bottom. I had the baby's breath cut, so all I had to do was place the roses in the tins of water and add the delicate, lacy white flowers. The daughters and daughter-in-law sat around my kitchen table, watching me arrange the flowers. The bouquet grew and grew into a beautiful thing to behold. As I tucked the last piece of baby's breath into place, we all looked at each other and fought back tears. The three young women paused to hug me as they headed out the door with the basket. We had all become a part of it. Javiel could finally be buried. Each of us found a little bit of peace.

The same day that Celina was crying with me about a funeral wreath, she was crying to Perfecto about Javiel not having a proper suit in which to be buried. Kind-hearted Perfecto told Celina not to worry, he would find something appropriate. He immediately called Pilar and told her to go through his clothes and find a suit and shirt for Javiel. Pilar was the kind of woman who would do that without hesitation. If that dead boy needed clothes, then clothes he would get. It was the right thing to do.

Perfecto also insisted that Celina choose a necktie, which was a little amusing since it was likely that no one in the Flores family had ever owned a necktie. Finally, together, Pilar and Celina worked out the burial attire for Javiel. Not only did the young man have a funeral spray, he was properly dressed for the occasion.

I went to the funeral and sat with the family in the small Evangelical church next to the railroad tracks. It was a moving experience, and the beautiful old basket full of red roses was the perfect touch. I was glad to be a part of the experience. The funeral was at ten in the morning, and I returned home directly after we had each thrown a handful of dirt on Javiel's casket as it was being lowered into the ground.

I spent the afternoon cooking a meal of *carne adovada* and beans to take to the dead boy's family. That evening, when I took the food to the Flores house, the back door was standing wide open. As I stepped inside, people began shouting, "Come in, come in," just as they had done the first time I had visited. It took a moment for my eyes to adjust to the darkened room, and then I realized that every person in the house was blind drunk, including the three young women.

The shock nearly knocked me over. For a little while, I had forgotten the real despair of that family. The level of their grief was wrenching, and the way in which they dealt with it, even more so for me. I left the pots of food on the table and slipped out the door, leaving them to their sorrow.

Every now and then, Celina came up to call the District Attorney's office and check on the progress of the murder case. Our friend Jack Slater was going to be the prosecuting attorney at the trial. We didn't envy him that job. The two defendants were of the lowest life caste in Santa Teresa. Whoever prosecuted in cases like those had to worry a bit about their personal safety. During another trial around the same time, a bomb had gone off in the District Attorney's office. It was a clear message from the supporters of the defendant. However, nothing so dramatic happened in Javiel's case.

Days passed as the legal process inched its way toward the actual trial date. On a hot fall day, Celina came up to make her final call to the office of the District Attorney. She listened for what seemed like a long time, her face a mask. Suddenly, Celina turned white and hung up the phone. She looked at me, or really through me, for a bit before speaking. "They got nine years," she said very quietly. "Nine years. With parole they will be out in three- for torture and murder-three years."

Her face turned to stone as she said, "One more phone call." She dialed the number, waited a little while, and then said, "They got nine years. That's three with parole. You know what to do. Good-bye."

Celina looked at me with narrowed eyes as she replaced the receiver. "I'll tell you this," she said in a quiet, controlled voice, "Those two will never live to finish their sentence."

The woman had a heart of gold, but beneath that veneer there beat a heart of steel. Celina opened my back door and headed down the driveway in her rubber thongs, a cigarette dangling from her right hand. I stood speechless, in total disbelief. It took a moment to realize, I had just witnessed justice in the Wild West.

16

Jeronimo

Jeronimo was a wild man who lived in a house down on the plaza when we first moved into San Ignacio. He called himself Jeronimo because he undoubtedly had Indian genes, and he did look more Native American than Hispanic. His hair was jet-black, thick and straight, fairly long and cut off bluntly. He wore a red bandana headband to complete the image. Jeronimo was on the short side, with extremely dark skin. He was also lean and wiry, and muscular from years of cutting and tossing firewood into piles. The guy wore the front of his shirt open, exposing his chest, which was smooth and hairless. Jeronimo walked with a lope, his arms swinging loosely at his sides, pausing slightly with each step. If the man was coming toward you, it all came off as a bit of a swagger.

Jeronimo seemed like an animated cartoon figure, especially at first, when we only saw him from the distance of our hill above the village. More accurately, we heard Jeronimo before we saw him. At that time, he drove a white van of '70s vintage. Every time he drank excessively, which was fairly often, he and his wife got into a fight. Then Jeronimo would jump in the van, put it in first gear and drive around the plaza in circles. Because he never put it in second or third gear, the engine sounded

Claudia Clavel

like a jet plane trying to take off. Whenever we heard that sound, we knew who it was. Jeronimo drove in circles until one or more of the tires went flat, and then he passed out over the steering wheel. The van sat where it had stopped until he woke up.

Thomas and I were always terrified that the madman would kill himself or someone else in the village, but he never did. It got to the point where we would never drive on the frontage road on Sunday afternoons, for fear of encountering Jeronimo head-on—literally. That fear came from experience. Once, we were coming down the hill into the river valley on that road, and heading right toward us, was the mad Jeronimo. He was hunched forward in the seat, both hands gripping the steering wheel as he careened from one side of the road to the other.

Some awareness on his part or luck on ours propelled him into the right lane, and we passed unscathed. Another Sunday afternoon, as we turned onto the dirt road into the village, there was Jeronimo, passed out in his van, which was tipped at a perilous angle on the side of the hill next to the road. It was best to let him be, for at that time, he was an unpredictable character.

When Jeronimo and I finally met face to face, it was when he came up to sell us a load of firewood. He knocked on the door, and as soon as I opened it, he said, "Hello, my name is Jeronimo, and I have a very hard life." He then launched into a story about somebody shooting the windows out of his van with a shotgun. He was trying to figure out how to retaliate—with me. The man had completely forgotten why he had come to my house. I started to laugh loudly and then said, "I'm sorry, but here you are, trying to work out a shooting problem with an Anglo woman you have just met."

Accidental Anthropologists

Standing there in front of me, with his shirt front open, wearing that headband, he looked at me in disbelief, and then started laughing heartily. "You're right, what was I thinking?" he replied. "So, do you want to buy some wood?"

"Sure," I answered. "Bring it up this evening, and Thomas will help you unload it." We bought wood from Jeronimo on a number of occasions after that, and he continued driving round and round in circles on most weekends until they moved away.

We didn't see Jeronimo again for several years. Him and his wife split up, and he was living in La Paloma, in a compound of family members.

Not too long after Javiel's funeral, which had become a topic in the valley because of my involvement in helping the family. That simple act, established our reputation among the people of the area, and especially our neighbors. Thomas and I were chatting with Celina and Lazaro Flores in the parking lot at La Tienda, where we all went for minor grocery items and movie rentals. We were talking about building projects, and Thomas mentioned needing *vigas*, the large log beams used in all the local adobe construction. There it was again, if you needed something, anything at all, the first thing you did was to let people know what you were looking for. It didn't matter whether it was appliances, eggs, adobes, or labor. You just put the word out, and before long, the right person or item turned up. So the word went out-*vigas*. Thomas needed *vigas*.

Sure enough, a few days later, a guy drove up to our place and beeped his horn. I went out to see who it was. The man was a dark-skinned local with a beard and mustache, and he was driving the oldest, most beat-up and battered pickup truck I'd ever seen. He had a bandana tied around his forehead and looked familiar, but I couldn't place him. I was surprised when he addressed me by name: "Mrs. Clavel, my name is Jacinto Gomez. Lazaro told me your husband is looking for *vigas*. I got the *vigas* he's looking for."

"Great," I replied. "How many do you have, and how much do you want for them?" He said, "I have ten *vigas*, sixteen feet long. I need a hundred and sixteen dollars to fix the engine in my other truck."

"Sounds like a deal to me," I replied. "My husband will come to your place this evening to check them out and give you the money."

Jacinto gave me directions to his house, and then lurched his truck backward down our rutted driveway. I went back inside, still sensing that I had seen the guy before. Thomas went later that day, gave Jacinto the cash, and explained that he didn't have a way of hauling the huge, heavy logs home. Jacinto said he didn't have a truck big enough to deliver them either, but no problem. The *vigas* could just remain where they were, until our neighbor Catarino had his big truck repaired. He owed Thomas a favor, so they would pick them up later when his truck was fixed. Jacinto told Thomas, "My mother will keep an eye on those *vigas* that are paid for in full." They shook hands on it.

When I told that story to Perfecto at the post office, and Thomas told it to Catarino, the two men couldn't stop laughing. They hooted and howled, taking turns saying, "You will never see those *vigas* again. Jacinto is the biggest crook in the valley. He's probably sold those *vigas* several times." Soon, the entire valley knew about Thomas buying *vigas* from Jacinto for cash but not bringing them home.

Accidental Anthropologists

The big truck belonging to Catarino was not repaired for a long time. Six months to be exact. Every time Catarino saw Thomas, he would ask about the *vigas*, "You think those logs are still there waiting for you?" and then howl with laughter. Finally, the truck was repaired, and Catarino drove up one morning to ask Thomas if he wanted to go pick them up. "Boy, Thomas, I can't wait to see your face when we drive up to that empty pile." It had become the valley joke; everyone was having a great time with it.

Off they drove to La Paloma and the house of Jacinto's mother. Thomas got out of the truck and walked to the front door, where he knocked and waited for her to answer. Catarino sat in the cab of his truck, watching, with a huge grin on his face.

Mrs. Gomez stepped out onto the porch, and Thomas introduced himself: "Hello, I'm Thomas Clavel. I bought some *vigas* from your son, Jacinto, and have come to pick them up. I'm sorry it's taken so long, Catarino just got his truck fixed."

Mrs. Gomez stepped back a bit and looked at Catarino sitting in the truck, and then at Thomas. She said, loudly enough for Catarino to hear, "Mr. Clavel, I'm so glad to see you. Jacinto told me to keep an eye on those *vigas*. He said, 'Don't let nobody near them, until Mr. Clavel comes to pick them up.' I've been watching those *vigas* for months. *Gracias a Dios*, now I can relax."

Thomas said later, "The look on Catarino's face was worth the wait!" It was an unbelievable act. Jacinto had been true to his word, and it had to do with Lazaro and Celina, and the funeral of their son. My simple act of kindness had made a big impression on the community and it would never be forgotten. As a result, it made our life a lot easier over the years. We would reap the benefits for years to come.

Claudia Clavel

It was the talk of the valley for a while. It made us think about honor and compassion, and a culture much different from our own. We felt lucky to be living in such a unique place. It certainly made us feel more a part of it. At the same time, I realized, Jacinto and Jeronimo, were one, and the same man. It would not be the last time we met people of duality in the valley.

Over time, Jacinto stopped drinking and became an animal rescue volunteer. A few years later, Thomas and I attended his wedding to Elvira. Not too long after the wedding, the four of us worked together as extras in a dance hall scene for a movie being shot in the area. Occasionally, throughout the years, we bumped into one another. Happily, Jacinto never did fall off the wagon, a real test of his strength in the valley.

17

Preciliano

Preciliano Medina had been the unofficial San Ignacio plumber for years. He worked for little or no pay, when the old rusted pipes of the village broke down. The man was also a scholar. Thomas told me that the first time he entered Preciliano's little adobe house, he was stunned to see bookshelves lining three walls, from ceiling to floor. The man didn't have running water or a bathroom. However, he had walls of books. Thomas said Preciliano handed him two books, and one was titled: *What the Philosophers Thought of God*. As Thomas slowly scanned the book titles, he became increasingly impressed by the guy's depth.

During that conversation, Preciliano told Thomas that he had become a more focused reader during his years in prison. Then he slowly began to tell his story. The same Preciliano: former tattoo artist at the State Pen in Santa Fe. The very same Preciliano Medina: ex-con, formerly of Leavenworth Federal Penitentiary, at Leavenworth, Kansas. He served five years for armed robbery. Sadly, Preciliano was also a chronic alcoholic and occasional heroin user. He was sixty years old, and afraid of dying! That surprised me, when he told me during a drive to Santa Teresa.

Claudia Clavel

Visually, Preciliano was the most colorful of all the Drinkers. A slightly built man, he was almost emaciated, with gaunt, sunken cheeks from years of not eating real food, relying on booze to sustain him. One of Preciliano's colorful aspects was the crocheted hat a girlfriend had made for him and which he was never seen without. The cap was a multi-colored band of stripes, going round and round, and it hugged the man's small head. Beneath the hat was a gray ponytail, held with a bright-colored elastic band. On the opposite side of his head, the man's chin sported an identical ponytail, with the same colored band. Preciliano walked very, very slowly, a little hunched over, as though he wasn't sure he really wanted to be going wherever it was he was headed. Whenever I encountered the man, I had to smile.

We hired Preciliano to help with some plumbing problems when we first moved to San Ignacio. He was extremely good at his craft and didn't charge enough, so we paid him more. He cut wood for us occasionally, and either Thomas or I would help stack while Preciliano chopped. On those occasions, we always had great conversations regarding everything to do with life in general. Besides being an intellect, Preciliano was a philosopher, with a great sense of humor. Like us, he loved the irony in life. Our neighbor was very open about his background; to him it was just part of the life process. Given his childhood with a physically abusive father, the guy hadn't stood much of a chance. According to Preciliano, he embraced the stimulation of criminal behavior early on.

We rarely saw Preciliano, except for the odd jobs that we were able to pass on. We enjoyed his company and extremely mellow behavior, and I would make a point of asking him in for a cup of coffee, just so we could chat a while longer.

Accidental Anthropologists

A couple of years after we had been living in San Ignacio, there were a bunch of break-ins within the village as well as in the surrounding area. It was usually a seasonal thing, early summer when wayfaring sons wandered back into the area. Most often, they had been in a drug rehab program out in California, or on the streets. However, they were always thinking about home. The other season was right before Christmas, when unemployment and SSI checks weren't quite enough during the giving season. That left a hard-core group of drinkers in the village that whiled away their days with cheap wine, Pabst Blue Ribbon beer and miniature bottles of hard liquor.

So during the time of break-ins, Preciliano showed up at our door one day to tell us straight out that we would never be "hit." His exact words were: "We, we want you to know, you will never be 'hit' as long as you live here." At first, we couldn't appreciate the impact of that statement, but as the years went by, we grew to understand the greater implication.

On one occasion, I encountered Preciliano coming from the post office, pushing a wheelbarrow. We both stopped for a moment as I remarked, "Whew, what a load of mail you have today."

"I wish they were all acceptance letters for my manuscripts," he replied. That was how I learned about his prolific writing habit. It turned out Preciliano had old, beat-up suitcases filled with handwritten manuscripts. He told me that every now and then, some knowledgeable person came along and attempted to help him get something published. Then, he would go off on one of his binges and never follow through. That had been a pattern for a long time, so things didn't look too hopeful.

Claudia Clavel

One scorching day in September, two days before I was going in for cataract surgery, I went down for the mail. When I stepped out the post office door, Preciliano was waiting for me, holding a bottle of beer in his hand. He slurred a bit, "Claudia, you're my friend, and you have to help me. I have to get to detox in Santa Teresa, and you will have to drive me there. I'm desperate."

All I could think about was the fifty-mile trip and a load of laundry in the washer. Not to mention all the other things needing attention before my surgery. I stood and looked at him a bit, then noticed he had the shakes. He was wearing a wool jacket, and it was hotter than blazes there in the mid-morning sun. He took a swig from the beer bottle, waiting for my answer. Very reluctantly, I agreed to drive him and made it clear I needed to be back as soon as possible. Preciliano led me to believe that he would be staying at the detox center for a few days. I told him I had to run home and organize a few things but would pick him up within fifteen or twenty minutes.

Preciliano was waiting for me when I drove up to his house. He called out, "Wait, I have to give the dog some water." As he entered the car, I looked in his eyes, trying to determine whether he had been doing heroin, as well as drinking. I couldn't tell. As we pulled out onto the frontage road, I noticed him pull a bottle of beer out of a jacket pocket. When we reached La Cantina bar next to the highway on-ramp, Preciliano hurled the empty beer bottle out his open window. I nearly slammed on the brakes, as I yelled at him, "What are you doing?" and then decided he was in no shape to be hassled.

After I pulled out onto the highway, I asked him if he was strung out on heroin. "No, no, no, beer only," he replied. "How long has this been going on?" I queried. "Two and a half months," he said, as he pulled another beer out of yet another pocket. "I'm in really bad shape," he went on. "If the doctor will just give me the medicine, I can do the detox myself."

"That doesn't seem very realistic," I responded.

As I drove on, I felt the need to ask Preciliano how he had started down that self- destructive path. He started to throw another empty bottle out the window, but I interrupted him. "Just put it on the floor," I said, rather sternly. Immediately he pulled another hidden bottle out of an inside pocket.

I did think about being pulled over by a cop and having to explain the situation, but by then, Preciliano had launched into his story of becoming a criminal. I asked about Leavenworth and how he wound up in the federal pen. He told me about an armed bank robbery involving a couple of other guys. He said the bank employee wouldn't open the safe, even with a gun held to his head. Preciliano said, "I kept telling the guy, 'Give me the money, man, it's not your money, just open the safe and give me the money.'"

Before we reached town, I would learn that Preciliano was addicted to: romance, sex, booze and the thrill of criminal behavior. He said he thought he had conquered heroin. Just then, we arrived in Santa Teresa, and I asked where the detox center was located.

"Well, actually, just drive me to my doctor's office and I'll see whether he can fit me in," he said. I parked nearly in front of the office door, and as Preciliano got out of the car, he set his bottle of beer in the shade, next to the open door. He came out a few minutes later, with news that the doctor couldn't see him until two.

"I'll just hang with you," he said. By then, I was pretty pissed, because it was about to drag on all afternoon. "No way," I responded. "I'm taking lunch to

Thomas at his shop, and you're too bombed to be in the middle of town."

"You're right," he said, not at all perturbed by my refusal. "Drive me to my friends, over in the barrio, and I'll wait for you there. You can pick me up a little before two."

I said, "OK, I'll drive you there, but you'll have to ride home with Thomas, because I have to get back."

While we were stopped at the intersection of Main and Columbia, waiting for a green turn light, a red car drove up on my right. A guy yelled, "Hey, bro, where you headed?" There were two or three guys in the car, apparently friends of Preciliano. I made my turn, and let Preciliano direct me to the house of his friends. It wasn't long before we were on a dirt road, way out on the west side of Old Town, near the cemetery.

Suddenly, I looked in the rear view mirror and realized we were being followed by an orange pickup truck. There were three men in the wide seat. I immediately pulled over, thinking, "If those are enemies of Preciliano, I want to know right now."

The orange truck pulled up next to the passenger side, and the driver yelled, "Hey, *compadre!*" Then somebody else yelled, "Bro, hey man, whacha doing out here?"

Preciliano told them his story, and the driver addressed me: "We'll take care of him now, ma'am. Don't worry, we'll get him to the doctor, and see that he gets home."

I felt relief surge through my body. Just before Preciliano got out of the car, he leaned over and kissed me on the cheek. "I'll never forget you for this. Thank you, thank you," he said. I thought about my new reputation in the city of Santa Teresa.

Accidental Anthropologists

As I found my way back out of the barrio, a wave of anger swept over me. By the time I got to Thomas's shop, I was angry that I was angry. Preciliano had conned me into taking him to town. The man had no real intent of getting himself cleaned up. I should not have been driving around that barrio with a known criminal who had as many enemies as friends. Besides, I never did learn whether he had shot the bank employee. He must not have; five years didn't seem like enough time for that crime.

Preciliano's friends didn't bring him home for a couple of days, and I knew for sure he never got to detox. That binge went on for another month or so. Thankfully, he never asked me to take him again. When Preciliano did finally enter the detox program, he got them to send a van to pick him up at his house. It didn't take long before the con man had the system figured out. You could almost hear sighs of relief in the village. I wasn't the only one he had been asking for rides over the years.

Eventually Preciliano moved to town and lived among friends. We bumped into him occasionally. He appeared more hunched over and emaciated than ever, but at seventy-six years of age, he was still hanging on. And we worried about eating bacon. Talk about irony.

Amazingly, the man lived long enough to have a full-page story of his life, including photographs, published in The Santa Fe New Mexican. A reporter learned about Preciliano's suitcases full of stories and interviewed him. Preciliano came to see us right after the publication to ask Thomas if he would publish his book. He was so excited by the attention and the thought of finally getting his story out there. Thomas asked him if someone had typed his hand-written notes, and he said a friend was working on it. Thomas told Preciliano to bring the typed manuscript to him when it was finished, and he would get his book published.

A few weeks later, Preciliano called us to ask whether he might stay in my studio for a few days. He said he needed a place to work on his book. Thomas was using the studio as an office for his Water Association work. As treasurer, he was in the middle of a massive project to get all the paper files into the computer. He was working with state and federal inspectors, trying to get everything caught up and to standards. Thomas didn't feel he could give up the space.

Within a week, we had a phone call informing us that Preciliano had died. It didn't take long for us to realize that Preciliano had wanted to come home to die, in the village where he was born. We were just happy that he had received some recognition for his intellect and writing skills.

18

Feliciano and Pita

Feliciano and Pita lived just below us in a singlewide mobile home, the roof covered with tires. Car tires. When they moved the singlewide onto their land, Feliciano hired a couple of young boys to cover the roof with good-size rocks. It wasn't long before the rocks returned to the ground. When the next big windstorm hit, Thomas and I heard lots of laughter as the rocks were heaved off the roof. The next day, at least a couple dozen tires appeared, where they remained until, eventually, a new pro-panel roof was added. San Ignacio was famous for its fierce winds that roared down from the northwest through the river valley almost all year long. Put a mobile home in the wind's path, and you can be guaranteed a jumping, undulating roof that will scare the pinto beans out of you.

On the day the tires were being hoisted up, Thomas hollered down the hill to Feliciano, "What happened to your rocks?"

"*Hijolo*, those rocks jumped up and down like popcorn when the big winds came. We had to run outdoors. The noise nearly made us deaf," Feliciano hollered back.

The old car tires just lay there, flat and snug. As hard as the wind has blown at times, I've yet to see a tire flying off any roof in the village.

Claudia Clavel

We had one tire on our roof for a while. Our tin roof was old and rusted, and over the years, some of the edges had come loose. There were so many nail holes in the tin it was hard to find a new place to drive a nail or screw.

During a particularly nasty storm, the roof on the northeast corner came loose. It was pouring rain, with the hint of hail in the air. Thomas ran out to fasten it down but couldn't find a nail space. I saw him running toward the cars, where he picked up a tire off the ground and then hie-tailed it back to the corner of the house. I heard a loud thump as the tire found its place on the roof. Thomas was laughing when he came in. "This is how it all begins: a tire here today, tomorrow another tire, until before you know it, your whole roof is covered with them," he said, still laughing.

The next ingenious addition to Feliciano and Pita's home was a cement block wall, installed right up against the west wall of the trailer. When the wind came blasting up out of the arroyos, it hit their trailer broadside, giving them quite a start. Pita made goat cheese to sell, and she said the wind's blasts made her spill her goat milk more than once, before that wall was installed. After that, they were in good shape wind-wise, and nothing jumped around.

I laughed out loud when Feliciano asked me, "Do you know how to tell when the wind stops blowing?"

"No," I replied. "Tell me."

"The chickens fall over," he answered.

Feliciano's passion was raising goats, chickens and rabbits, and whistling while he worked. Somehow, he coaxed a flock of pigeons away from the church steeple where they had lived for years, and into a pigeon coop he constructed for them. It had a trapdoor made of chicken wire that he opened at different times of the day, so the birds could go soaring over the village. Hawks and owls picked off the birds on a fairly regular basis, so the door was designed to keep predators from getting to the pigeons once they returned from their outings. Those birds seemed to know just how good their lives were, living with Feliciano and Pita.

Thomas and I loved watching the pigeon flock dipping and soaring over the village. We set up a log porch swing in our front yard, so we could sit out there in late afternoon in order to enjoy the sight. The birds flew in unison, down into the deep arroyo that runs into the river, and then came swooping upward right in front of us. For a few months one year, we had a pair of cockatiels that Thomas taught to fly.

The bird's wings had been clipped, and we didn't think about them growing back. When they did, Thomas spent time every day holding one finger out where the bird could perch. Each day, Thomas held his finger a bit further from the window ledge, chanting, "jump, jump." The little birds grew very excited, and they did begin to make progress

One day, one of them flew to the bird trainer from the window ledge, and the next day they were flying the length of the porch. From that day forward, the cockatiels were in love with my husband. The minute he returned from work, the birds flew to him and grabbed onto his shirt. One of them worked its way up to Thomas' chin and began kissing him on the mouth. The other bird hopped to the watch on Thomas' wrist and in the blink of an eye, pulled all the pins out of the watchband. Village children came up to visit the birds. They loved sitting on the porch holding one or both of the birds on their fingers.

The birds had the run of our long, glassed-in front porch and used to run along the window ledge. They seemed to be watching the pigeons during their outings, as they soared over the edge of our hill. One day, Thomas opened the door to step out just as one of the cockatiels landed on his head. The instant the door was opened, that bird took off, heading for the pigeon flock. Thomas hollered for me, and I joined him in the yard.

We stood, our mouths opened in amazement and horror, as the little tame bird joined the pigeon flock and flew in formation over the village, making several passes. During the entire flight, the other cockatiel was running madly back and forth on the porch window ledge. Just when we thought the escape artist was surely doomed, the bird suddenly appeared, landing on Thomas's shoulder. We have never been sure which of us looked more surprised. Within a few months, we gave the birds to a poet friend in Santa Teresa who had a bird aviary in his living room. Thomas couldn't take anymore bird kisses and watch demolition.

Feliciano constructed an adobe chicken house that eventually slid down the steep embankment on his *ranchito*. It was a nice touch though, since the adobe kept the chickens cool during summer and warm in winter. He built the rabbit hutches beneath the pigeon coop, so they would be out of the sun during hot summer months. The goats had a little barn-like shelter and otherwise wandered around with the chickens, and for a while with a horse, that someone had given Feliciano. The horse was a mare that had recently given birth to a foal. That was just before Oliver Stone came to direct a scene for "Natural Born Killers" in the village.

The day before the movie shoot, somebody shot the mare. Horses had wandered the village for years, foraging for grass and whatever else was available; you could count on it to happen, especially once spring arrived. We had fenced out local livestock from the beginning, and it was always a pain in the rear having to open and close gates, but we accepted it as a way of life. However, no one had ever shot a horse or cow before. It sent a few shock waves through the village for a while.

On the day of the movie chase scene, I was standing on our hill, watching the action in the plaza below. My gaze was pulled toward Feliciano's place, as I saw him hook something to the back of his pickup truck. He got in the cab and began driving very slowly out of his yard. As he came around the curve, I saw with horror that he was pulling the dead mare behind his truck, heading up the back road to the dump area. He was driving through the edge of the movie scene, and no one noticed, except for a few neighbors and me. But it didn't seem to disrupt the filming at all.

Then, there was the problem of the newborn foal that had lost its mother. It refused to drink from a bottle. Both Feliciano and Pita had a special way with animals, but even with all their coaxing, that baby refused to drink from the bottle.

I had listened to Feliciano whistling every morning and evening, from the time he set up his little *ranchito*, and it was one of the most comforting things in my life. With the birth of the foal, his whistling had taken on an especially joyful tone as he buzzed around down there, feeding his animals.

One evening, I walked to the edge of our hill and looked down. What I saw nearly sent me over the steep drop: There was Feliciano, holding a goat by a rope around its neck. The goat was standing on an old wooden table, and beneath the goat was the foal, its head upturned in order to reach the goat's teat. Feliciano had taught the baby horse to nurse from one of his she-goats.

Once in a while, the goat tried to kick the foal, but Feliciano hollered, "Hey, you behave." And the goat always did, and nursed that baby until it was old enough to eat solid food.

At Feliciano's request, Thomas went down to videotape the event, because Pita and Feliciano thought they could send it to "America's Funniest Home Videos." However, once they realized they would have to fly to L.A. if it was accepted, they panicked. They asked us to go for them, in case it was picked, but that wasn't our thing either, so nothing ever came of it. We still have a copy of the tape.

Feliciano and Pita were two of the happiest people we had ever met, in spite of a lot of obstacles in their lives. They both suffered diabetes with complications, he had been losing his eyesight for a long time, and it grew worse by the year. Feliciano was nearing fifty when they moved into the village, and he was always busy. He was on the short side, with a very round torso. He moved around slowly, swinging his body from one side to the other when he walked, due to a wooden peg leg that gave him fits occasionally.

When he built a wood porch on the east side of their house, Feliciano got the leg caught in a crack that pulled him down to the floor. Pita had gone somewhere, so he had to lie there until one of his friends happened along. Since the fall had broken the wooden leg, he had to hop along with the help of crutches for a while, until the leg had been repaired. He always laughed in telling that story and would end with, "Where were you, when I needed you?"

None of his problems ever stopped Feliciano from whistling once he stepped outdoors. One of my favorite experiences with our friend was hanging over the back of

Accidental Anthropologists

his pickup truck in front of the post office for a catch-up on our lives. Pita almost never left the house, so if I hadn't been down there for a while, I had to get all the news from Feliciano.

Pita was a remarkable woman in many ways. She was about to turn forty, short and stocky, with stiff, arthritic fingers. Sometimes, they were red and swollen from arthritis attacks. In spite of the pain, Pita usually had a smile extending to her chubby cheeks and seemed genuinely happy. She was constantly sewing wonderful creative things, some to sell, but more often, useful clothing items as gifts for her children and grandchildren. She sewed until her fingers locked up but said she was just happy to still be able to do it.

On a sunny fall afternoon when I went down to visit, I found Pita nearly in tears. She had been piecing a baby quilt on her sewing machine, and all of a sudden, the machine jammed and stopped dead in its tracks. Pita kept her composure as she told me the machine was less than a year old. Getting repairs required a fifty-mile round trip to town and then days of waiting while the guy found the source of the problem.

I told Pita that Thomas had taught me to service my own sewing machine, and she perked up at that news. I asked for a screwdriver and set about taking the machine apart. Just as I had expected, the feed-dog was packed with thread. A big mass had lodged beneath the plate. I took a large, heavy needle and began picking threads out of the mess. Once I had it cleared, I ran home for sewing machine oil and gave the machine a lube job. Within a couple of hours, that machine ran like a brand-new model. I showed Pita how to clean and oil the machine, so she could be forever free of repairmen.

Claudia Clavel

When Feliciano came in from outdoors, Pita could hardly wait to share the exciting news. "She's been crying over that sewing machine ever since it stopped. It's her baby. I can't believe you fixed it!" he nearly shouted. We were all feeling pretty good by then. "What do we owe you?" they asked simultaneously.

"Nothing, I'm just glad I was able to fix it," I replied. Feliciano went to the freezer and pulled out several wrapped packages. As he handed them to me, he said, "We just butchered rabbits. Here are a couple, and a big beefsteak. It's the least we can do for you." I thanked them for their generous payment and headed home.

About a week later, Thomas was in the post office when a *viejito* named Amado walked up to him. The old man asked, "You're married to the woman up on the hill, no? The Anglo woman who fixes sewing machines?"

"Yes, I am," replied my spouse.

"Well, *señor*, you got yourself a fine woman. She fixed my daughter's machine, and that thing runs like new. Yes, sir, you got yourself a fine woman up there."

"I sure do," replied my husband. "I'm a lucky man!"

There was a time when Pita took care of her daughter Carmen's little boy while Carmen worked in Santa Fe. Babysitting started from the time Pancho was born, and the grandmother told me it was a very trying time for her. She hadn't been around babies for a very long time and felt overwhelmed. However, after about three months, both she and Feliciano had adjusted to the huge change. By then, they were having the time of their lives, as the little boy cooed and gurgled his way into their hearts.

By the age of two, Pancho was a happy toddler on the little *ranchito*. I could see the child down below, following Feliciano around the animal yard, learning the fine arts of goat milking and egg gathering.

Accidental Anthropologists

Feliciano's eyesight eventually succumbed to total blindness. He was never quite able to resign himself to just sitting in a big, old chair on their enclosed front porch, waiting for some of his cronies to stop by for a visit. And they did. He was fortunate to have a steady stream of visitors on a daily basis. I tried to pop in at least once a week to pick up eggs and have a chat with him and Pita. During the afternoons, Feliciano took to sitting in the sun on their little back porch, which looked out on the road into the village. Feliciano could tell who belonged to every car that drove in and out by the sound of the engine. As he waved, as he did to every car, he also yelled at cars to slow down if they were going too fast. They usually did.

On a warm Sunday morning, Thomas was working in the front yard when he heard Pita's screams. She was in the goat pen when she saw Thomas up above her. He tore down the hill and into their yard, where he found Pita standing next to Feliciano, who was lying on the ground with a goat standing on his chest. Thomas knew immediately that Feliciano was dead, and told Pita to call 911. He took off his shirt and sat on the ground, cradling Feliciano's head in his lap. Thomas covered our friend's face with his shirt to keep the flies off and just sat waiting, until the family began to arrive. Pita had been at church, and Thomas figured Feliciano suffered a massive heart attack about an hour before Pita arrived. We all agreed that he had died just where he wanted to be: with his beloved animals surrounding him.

Shortly after the funeral, I was out in the yard when I heard the most wonderful sound coming from below. I looked down over the edge into Pita's animal pens, and there was Pancho, the grandson, who was by then about six years old. The young boy and his grandmother had begun taking over Feliciano's chores when his health started deteriorating. Little by little, the young boy had assumed all the responsibilities. There he was, alone, moving slowly among the chickens and goats, distributing their feed. And he was whistling. Not quite the same as his grandfather, but whistling, the entire time he moved around.

19

Jury Foreman

It was the first time Thomas had ever been called for jury duty. Early on a Monday morning, he sat in the county courthouse with a group of people from all walks of life, waiting for the process of elimination to take place. The trial was about a drug bust, and the defendant a neighbor of ours from a nearby village. The attorneys asked each person a series of questions, including his or her views on drug laws. Thomas had always believed in education and counseling, rather than incarceration. He was surprised to find himself not only chosen by the lawyers, but, a while later, picked as foreman of the jury.

The first day of the trial, Thomas sat looking out at the audience seated in the courtroom, and realized they were pretty much all our neighbors. Most of them were related to Filadelfio Mondragon, the defendant. Thomas said he had to wonder about his own future popularity in the community, if Filadelfio were to be found guilty of possessing forty pounds of marijuana with intent to sell.

Right before Filadelfio's arrest, an undercover agent in Alamo had stopped his nephew for speeding. When the officer found a small bag of pot on the seat, he wanted to know where it came from. The seventeen-year old boy had a sixteen-year old girlfriend and their baby in the car with him. The undercover agent intimidated the boy into naming the source of the marijuana, with the threat of putting him away, where he would never see the baby or girlfriend again. The boy cracked and named his uncle Filadelfio as the supplier.

Shortly afterward, Filadelfio was picked up at La Tienda while putting air in his tires. A baggie containing one joint was found beneath his car, and he was taken back to his house, where a search took place. Nothing was found inside Filadelfio's house, but they did find something in a nearby shed with several houses around it. In Filadelfio's village, houses were clustered close together. Many were little outbuildings that had been used for butchering animals or storing canned goods. The shed could have belonged to any number of people in that compound. That was important, because, inside the shed, the police found forty pounds of marijuana. Because his nephew had named Filadelfio, the police hauled him off to jail until a bail bond was posted.

A couple of major points were established during the first days of the trial: (1) when the police went to the shed, they found no footprints to or from Filadelfio's house. That was especially evident due to a blanket of snow covering the ground at the time. (2) They found no key to the shed in Filadelfio's home. In fact, they found no connection linking him to the shed at all.

Curiously, during the trial, the major discovery was the fact that the forty-pound bag of marijuana actually now weighed only twenty-eight pounds. According to local police, confiscated drugs went into a locked safe at the police station. However, the Drug Task Force had taken the forty-pound bag of pot to their office to be weighed and videotaped. Then they put it in an unlocked closet, where it languished for three weeks. When queried about the weight discrepancy, the detective stated, "It must have dried out."

When the plastic baggie found beneath Filadelfio's car was introduced as evidence, the joint was missing. According to Thomas, the lawyer actually held up an empty baggie, asking the Drug Enforcement officer, "Is this the baggie you found at the scene of the arrest?" By then, it was evident to Thomas that the police did not have a very tight case.

When the jury went into deliberations, Thomas noticed three jurors who seemed intent on convicting Filadelfio, regardless of guilt or innocence. One juror kept shouting, "Just look at the guy, he's got drugs written all over his face." Another juror wanted to convict in order to make a statement about drugs. Thomas was stunned by the concept of justice in some people's minds.

A small amount of marijuana had been confiscated at Filadelfio's house, supposedly the same amount as the nephew had when he had been stopped. If it didn't match the forty pounds, then it came from somewhere else. So the jury discussion became focused on the forty pounds versus the small amount. Thomas knocked on the door, calling for the bailiff to bring in all the pot so the jury could go through the bags, sniffing their way to a consensus. A juror next to Thomas whispered, "Hey, did anybody bring papers?" The sequestered jurors roared with laughter. With the exception of the three dissenters.

After a considerable amount of time spent smelling their way through bags of marijuana, the jurors were unable to link, by odor, the large amount of weed to the small amount found in Filadelfio's house. It was now obvious to the majority of the jury that the whole case was one big botch-up by both the Drug Task Force and the local police. Nine jurors felt they had no choice but to vote not guilty. The three dissenters voted for a guilty verdict. As a result, it was declared a hung jury. It was then up to the District Attorney to decide on another trial or to dismiss the case for lack of concrete evidence. Filadelfio was released. Case dismissed.

The week after the trial, I went down to buy eggs from Pita and Feliciano. As always, we settled in for some visiting and gossip. I told them about Thomas and the trial. Pita quipped, "Oh yeah, Chato's my cousin, that's his nickname, we have been really concerned for him. Chato is such a sweet guy, the only reason he would ever sell pot would be to help his dad. His mother died last year, and now his dad has brain cancer. He is the only one, out of all his brothers, who ever helped his parents. We're really glad he didn't do it. Chato doesn't deserve a jail sentence."

A few months later, we decided it was time to tile the front porch. There were five hundred hexagonal and small rectangular quarry tiles that we had bought from friend's years before, and we needed someone to set them for us. I asked Perfecto when I went down for the mail, "Do you know who does the best tile work in the area?"

He thought a moment and then replied, "Filadelfio Mondragon, over in San Pasqual." Once again, I laughed at the irony of our life in San Ignacio. I wrote Filadelfio's telephone phone number on a piece of paper and tossed it on the kitchen table.

That evening, when Thomas returned from work, he noticed the paper. "What's that for?" he asked. "Oh, it's the number for the tile setter, your old defendant, Filadelfio Mondragon."

"Good thing the guy was acquitted," muttered my spouse, "or we might be paying a lot more for the job."

20

Chato Mondragon

When we finally met Filadelfio, he introduced himself to us as Chato. He was a short, stocky guy, in his early thirties, built like a bulldog. His large head was set on his shoulders without a neck.

He had a beer belly that started just below his breastbone and swung down to the top of his thighs. Chato's short, beefy legs held it all up. The man's hands were massive, with fat, stubby fingers, most of which were covered with little cuts and bruises. That wasn't surprising, because Chato was a "rock man." The guy was as strong as an ox from harvesting green moss rock and various shades of flagstone during the summers.

The valley was known for its rock harvesters. You could see them year round, parked along the frontage road in Santa Fe. Their pickup trucks were lined up side by side, each with various sizes and shapes of freshly harvested rock and stone. It was the location where Santa Fe locals shopped for stacking rocks, boulders and flagstone to enhance their xeriscape projects. Chato was a hit with that crowd, because of his birdbath rocks. He was known for harvesting the best water rocks in the area.

Birdbath rocks are generally flat, and some are huge, with natural basins eroded by water rushing over them when they had been at the bottom of some ancient river. Chato showed up at our place a number of times to present some of his latest finds. We had very little money in those early days, but he made sure we could afford at least one birdbath rock.

On one occasion, he brought three small, graduated sizes that he thought would look good beneath our bird-feeder. When Chato delivered the rocks, he insisted that he dig a space where they would be placed, so he could nestle them in and make it appear they had always been there. He was that kind of guy, because Chato was also an artist. The rock man appreciated other people's talents, so for him, bringing us raw materials made him part of our creative process. It was something we would share for many years.

When Chato came to look at our porch tile project, we agreed on a price for laying the five hundred tiles. Thomas and I had carefully measured the space, so we knew we had enough tiles to complete the job. The tile set-ter became excited by the thought of laying the tiles in a key pattern to enhance the length of the porch, and he immediately jumped into the project. Before I realized what was happening, Chato had set the first tiles in place. I knew there weren't enough rectangular tiles for his plan, but for some reason, I didn't stop him. Probably, because I, too, trusted other people's artistic skills. However, that was my downfall, for it set off a chain of events that would dominate our life for a while.

The key design that Chato had firmly planted in his mind was far from our original floor plan of hexago-nal tiles with a simple border of rectangular tiles. Chato's design required many more rectangles than we had on hand. The worst part was the fact that he had begun cut-ting hexagonal tiles into rectangles. Thomas and I searched for red quarry rectangle tiles that would match what we had. We did find some, but Thomas wound up helping Chato mutilate the hexagons, so there would be enough. It went on much too long. At one point, I wanted to wring Chato's non-neck, but by then, the project was drawing to a close, and it would soon be over.

On his last day of work, there was a shout from Chato as he was laying the last tiles. He held up a rectangular tile with a printed image of St. Francis of Assisi. How it got there was a mystery, because all the others were blank. Both of us were stunned and had a good laugh. We took it as a sign that the job would work out fine. As it turned out, the key pattern designed by Chato Mondragon fit the porch perfectly, but if asked, I wouldn't know how to describe it. We never paid Chato more than his original bid, even though the job went on forever. But it didn't seem to matter to him, for he was having the time of his life, being creative with that key design he had in his head.

Chato did another job for us that prevented me from pitching a month's worth of hard labor. Our potter friend, Douglas, talked us into making and hand-painting tiles for our kitchen counter. He rolled out the clay and cut them into 300 tile shapes. Thomas did the white glaze work and I painted 100 border tiles in three colors to match kitchen chairs that I had designed a few years earlier. The three of us worked for a month, and when the final glaze firing was finished, to my eyes, the colors hadn't turned out right, and I didn't think I could live with the result.

Chato stopped by to give us a price for the tile-setting job, and when I showed him my disaster, he easily came up with a clever idea. I had the intended color of grout to use, so he found a cardboard box and turned it upside down. He set out eight tiles on the box bottom and then mixed the grout, which he applied between each tile. He assured me the grout color would pull it all together.

Chato drove off to do some errands and returned a couple of hours later when the grout had dried. He had been right. I was amazed, but he just smiled and said he knew I would be happy with the end result.

Because Thomas had watched and learned from Chato during the tile-setting process, he wound up doing a lot of the finish work on the counter. He would eventually go on to greater tile creations by himself.

When Chato needed a few bucks after spending the day in Santa Fe but not selling any rock, he would show up at our place. Usually with a load of flagstone, brick or stacking rocks. He would be hoping to sell them to us for such a reasonable price that we couldn't turn him down. Hauling a ton of rock nearly one hundred miles a day added up fast at the gas pump. On those occasions, we talked about how we were helping each other. There was a time we traded our old, great-running Jeep Cherokee to Chato for enough lavender flagstones to create a series of walks in front of our house. Thanks to the rock man and his hard labor, over the years we were able to create brick paths, flagstone walks, a couple of patios and a lovely, high, curved stacked-stone wall that linked two of our buildings together.

Thomas and I were lucky to have Chato come into our lives early in our time in the village, for it wouldn't be too many years later that his back finally gave out from all the summers of heavy lifting. It was after the kitchen counter job that Chato gave up his rock-harvesting and tile-setting career for less demanding work. He became a home health-care worker for a brother with debilitating health issues.

Accidental Anthropologists

Ever the artisan, Chato then took up stone carving on a small scale. He would show up in our driveway out of the blue, toot his horn and wait to share with us a few of his latest endeavors. The man was always filled with enthusiasm for whatever he was creating at the time. The overriding theme for Chato's stone sculptures was religious based, and most were small crosses. We were invariably surprised by the variety of colored stones he came up with and the ways he found to display them. Through the years, we were especially touched by the fact that he still wanted to share his art with us.

21

Cleo the Stone Man

As fate would have it, Cleo turned up in our life shortly after Chato retired from harvesting rock. He didn't live in San Ignacio but spent a lot of time in the village because of a little girl named Dawn. Cleo was Dawn's father. The child lived with her mother and grandparents. Rosina and Claudio Archuleta cared for their granddaughter while her mother worked two jobs in Santa Fe. Over the years, and another child, Cleo became a part-time fixture in the Archuleta household.

Cleo was in his late thirties when we started doing business with him. He was a wood seller, plasterer, carpenter and all-around handyman. Cleo was also a very skilled and creative stonemason. By the time, we met him, our acre of land was strewn with plenty of raw materials for someone like Cleo: piles of river rocks, stacking rocks and an assortment of flagstones we had acquired over the years. Finally, we had money to pay someone to do the work for us.

Thomas and I had hired Cleo in the past for various plastering jobs, so we knew he was a good worker. We also liked him personally, because we shared an interest in the creative process. Every now and then, Cleo showed up with a piece of woodwork he had created out of scrap materials. The pieces were always inventive, often with a sense of whimsy about them.

We bought a crude shelf he had made and decorated with large metal upholstery tacks. He had incised little marks around each tack to give the appearance of a "tucked and rolled" effect. We set a large wire-and-plaster, antique Mexican tree of life on the shelf, and Cleo's motif lent itself perfectly. It also made you smile to look at it.

One early summer morning, the artisan showed up at our door holding a curved table leg that was painted green. He said his mother had told him to throw it on the woodpile, but he thought I might be able to use it.

Incredibly, the day before, Thomas had asked me what kind of leg I wanted for the end of a low shelf that he had built along two walls in our new powder room in the casita. The shelf ended near the toilet, and the corner edge was suspended in space. There were many little square tiles in three pale earth tones around the lavatory and covering the long shelf, so I thought a few curves might be a nice contrast. Thomas said, "I don't do curvy legs. I only do square legs." We had let it go at that.

When Cleo showed up with that green table leg, we all started laughing as I exclaimed, "That's it!" I had already painted the powder room door a deep green, so all I had to do with the leg was sand it a little and it matched perfectly. Thomas simply cut off a three-inch piece at the bottom of the leg and screwed the top to the shelf. Our life has always worked like that.

Cleo was of medium height, lean and wiry. He was a good-looking guy and strong, in the way that Thomas was strong. Both men had reputations for their skills in moving massive objects by themselves. They were strategists in that sense, and you could see them thinking about the problem and then watch as they worked it out. I was stunned when Cleo moved huge slabs of river-bottom rock fifty feet across the yard to where he would set them in place. Most of the slabs weighed over a hundred pounds, and I have never been sure how he did it.

Over time, our flagstone piles found their way to a series of walks in front of the house. Cleo was a master stonecutter, and all the pieces fit together perfectly. He insisted on cementing the joints, so we wouldn't have to be sweeping gravel around the walks. Thomas and I especially appreciated Cleo's design element when he put the walks together. He used slight curves and odd angles to create interesting effects in all his stonework.

After the walkways were done, we still had mounds of building stones and knew we wanted another project. Once again, we contacted Cleo.

We wanted a curved wall of stacked stones to run between the house and the sunroom. When we asked Cleo to build the wall, he said, "I don't know how to build a stacked wall. Why don't I use cement and attach rock to the face?"

San Ignacio had a number of stacked stone buildings, and we thought them incredibly beautiful. I told Cleo, "You go walking along the back road and take a look at those stone houses. I'm sure you will see how it is done. And Thomas will help you get started."

Once Cleo got the foundation poured and several steel rods set in place for stability, he was ready to start stacking stones. We had piles to choose from, so he started with the large ones for the foundation. Then things started to get interesting as he felt his way along. At one point, I found him cutting scrap flagstone into useable pieces. He had already spent a few hours cutting and stacking the thin stones. We were paying him by the hour and I started getting nervous about the time involved.

I asked him to move on to larger stones and then suggested Thomas work with him to speed things up.

The next morning Cleo had already started work when Thomas went out. I joined him and something made us hesitate. We stood together on the *portal* for a moment watching Cleo. He was holding a stone in his hand, and he was talking to it. Without a hint of self-consciousness, the young man turned toward us and said, "I've been asking this guy where he wants to live in the wall. I think I know where he wants to be, and I'm going to put him there now."

Thomas looked at me, and I nodded as he said, "Cleo, we think you know better than we do just how the wall should be built. And it looks like you don't need a helper."

The wall grew to around six feet high, creating a sheltered courtyard fifteen feet across between the buildings. It cost us a little more to get the job done. But everyone who sees that wall stops to admire the beauty of the thoughtfully crafted work of art. It's the most beautiful thing Cleo built for us.

22

Hilario the Burrito Man

Hernandez Ranch was a sparsely populated, sprawling community, with no real center. It was located on top of Maxwell Mesa, and you got there by driving up a winding road that forked off the little blue highway that ran through the valley. Once you passed the valley elementary school and blacktop, it was about a fifteen-mile drive on gravel to the top. Still considered a Spanish Land Grant, the original ranch had been chopped up into varying sized parcels. Some were subdivided for upscale homes, but most of the plots were little *ranchitos*, inhabited by natives of the area. Locals eked out a subsistence living as ranchers, rock harvesters and wood gatherers.

Hilario the Burrito Man was born on Hernandez Ranch and lived there with his wife, Elvira. He made the long drive every morning to make his burrito rounds throughout the valley. The man drove that road all year, rain or snow. Frequently, the towering mesa had its own weather, so the burrito salesman never knew what he might be heading into on his drive home.

He got up at 5 a.m. to make the flour tortillas that were the base for his burritos. Every day, Hilario surprised himself with the ingredients he chose. I think his choices often had to do with his customers, for we all had our favorites. The man was adamant about customer satisfaction. The burrito circuit rider had a special relationship with each customer. I wasn't the only one who looked forward to his deliveries. Hilario shared something special with each of us.

The Burrito Man drove up our driveway nearly every day with the day's selections. He always said, "Today I have your favorite burrito. You know, the one with red chile, potatoes and corned beef." How could I refuse such an offer, when it was so personal? Hilario's burritos cost a dollar fifty each, a bargain when you realized the price asked by his retail customers at the local bars. A great bargain when you remembered they were delivered to your door.

He kept the burritos warm in a Coleman ice chest on the floor behind the driver's seat of his long, beat-up 1970's Dodge sedan. Sometimes, Hilario and I chatted for a while, other times not at all. On those occasions, we simply exchanged greetings, burritos and money, in one brief transaction. The man told me right from the start that I should never invite him inside my home. He said he could never be trusted, once he knew the contents of the interior, for he was, at heart, a hopeless thief.

With every delivery, Hilario had a story to tell or some information to be shared. Over time, as I got to know the man, the more I appreciated his native intelligence and the humanity he showed for all those around him. When I told Hilario about my brother's malignant brain tumor, without a word, he stepped out of the car and bowed his head in front of me. I nearly fell over, until Hilario finally began to speak. He said, "Feel the front of my head, here," and with that, he took hold of my right hand and placed it on his head.

Accidental Anthropologists

My first awareness was of how thick his hair was, and then suddenly I felt it—a huge dent in his skull. I jerked my hand back, sort of horrified. I said, "Oh my God, what is that?"

Hilario told me about his brain tumor, and how they had to cut away part of his skull. Since he had obviously survived, his story did give me hope for my brother. It also made me more aware of how hope was passed around in the valley. It was done in the form of stories. And it happened all the time.

During another burrito delivery, Hilario told me about making money on wagers regarding his ability to carry a one-hundred-pound sack of flour or grain with his teeth. He told me he used to do it a lot, but now that he was growing older, only occasionally. When I asked Hilario how far he could carry a one-hundred-pound sack of flour, he pointed to a distance that would appear to be about fifteen or twenty feet. He said he always won, and the onlookers were amazed by his strength. The work Hilario did at that time apparently trained him well: he stacked or unloaded one-hundred-pound bags of cement onto and off semis, eight hours a day for a lot of years.

When Hilario drove up our long driveway, he always parked right in front of the kitchen door and started revving the engine of his Dodge. He drove a couple of different cars, but neither of them had a horn. He had to rev the engine to get your attention. The man never got out of his car to knock on the door. At least part of that ritual had to do with dogs. Many yard dogs were deliberately menacing, and that's why people honked when they drove into someone's yard. The only problem with Hilario's announcement was: if you happened to be in the laundry room or bathroom, you didn't hear the engine rev. In that case, you both lost out. It was a sad fact that I contributed very little to Hilario's income. The amount of gas he used revving his engine probably put him close to the red mark on his income sheet when he was selling burritos to me.

One summer morning, around 9:30, Hilario drove up and revved the engine. When I went out to greet him, I was amused to see three other guys in the car. In the back seat, there was Macario, with a big toothless grin, holding a small ice chest on his lap. Next to him sat Preciliano, with his ponytail beard, wearing a very cool pair of sunglasses. The guy sitting next to Hilario in the front seat was someone I had never seen before. That prompted me to think about the number of people Hilario had shown up with, whom I had never laid eyes on. Which was somewhat surprising, when I thought about how sparsely populated the valley was.

I stood a moment, taking in the scene of the big old Dodge filled with morning cruisers. The smell of fresh burritos wafted out the windows. I started to laugh as I said, "You guys remind me of one of those 'how many men does it take to...?' jokes. So, how many men does it take to deliver a burrito?"

They each had an answer: Macario said, "One to hold an ice chest on his lap." Preciliano continued, "One to open the lid." Without a pause, the guy in front went on, "One to pass the beer." Hilario kind of snorted as he added, "Hey, it takes just one. The others are along for company." We all shared a good laugh. At times like those, I wished I were a photographer, for it would have been a great shot. I paid for my burrito as Hilario, ever the salesman, said, "By the way, I have your favorite tortillas today."

Hilario sometimes bagged up a dozen or so extra tortillas to sell. I could never turn those down, for they were truly incredible. The price was two-fifty a dozen, a little pricey at the time, but definitely worth the extra money. However, that particular day, I didn't have two-fifty and wouldn't until the following day. Hilario's response was, "Hey, tomorrow is almost here, no problem. I'll drop by then."

The next day happened to be Friday the thirteenth. I was out doing yard work when Hilario drove up with yet another new face. I had the two-fifty in my pocket and met them in the middle of the driveway.

I handed the money to Hilario and said, "No burrito for me today." His reply was to hand me a burrito as he said, "Yes, you are having a burrito. This is Friday the thirteenth, and that scares most people, but not me. I woke up this morning, and the Man Upstairs said this was going to be a good burrito day for me, so I'm feeling charitable."

I took the offering gratefully as Hilario went on, "You would probably have more money to spend, if I didn't keep coming up here, trying to sell you burritos." He was dead serious, and I was greatly moved by his sensitivity. There were times when I had to raid the change box and found myself down to pennies.

I swear, I didn't know how some conversations came about. But every now and again, there I would be, discussing the most bizarre subjects with him. In one case, it was hemorrhoids. Holding a warm burrito in my hand, I stood there, talking about hemorrhoids with Hilario. He was telling me about a home remedy that he insisted worked wonders. An old woman somewhere down the valley made the concoction for him. The *curandera* insisted Hilario gather the ingredients for the salve out in the juniper and piñon forest. The Burrito Man said he would bring me a sample on his next trip up my driveway. I knew he would, for when Hilario had a mission, he never forgot.

Claudia Clavel

Sure enough, Hilario was back the next morning, revving his engine in front of my door. When I stepped out into the blinding sun, he had already rolled the car window down. He instructed me to bring two small squares of aluminum foil and a spoon. I was already laughing by the time I fulfilled his request. Hilario turned in his seat to reach a jar sitting on the back seat of his car. His face became very serious as he unscrewed the lid and held the jar out for me to take. "Smell it," he ordered, in his mild-mannered way. The odor was piñon, quite pleasant, not at all what I had expected. "Now," he instructed, "take a spoonful, and put one on each piece of foil."

I had to set everything on a stump next to the porch door in order to perform the operation. When the small mounds of ointment were in the right positions, Hilario told me to begin rolling the foil over the salve and to continue rolling until it was in a tight little packet. He said it should look like a hand-rolled cigarette. The Burrito Man watched me until I had both pieces rolled.

"Now then, you put those in the refrigerator to chill, and you're ready for the first signs of hemorrhoids. I guarantee that cool piñon will be just what the doctor ordered," he cooed.

"Hilario, what would we do without you," I laughed. "Imagine, hot burritos and cool suppositories, all in the same delivery. What a guy."

Right around Christmas time, Hilario brought us a container of *sopa*, a bread pudding made with white bread, *piloncillo* (a Mexican brown sugar in a cone shape), yellow cheese and raisins. The *sopa* he brought also had almonds, a nice touch. *Sopa* was almost always served during the holidays and special occasions. Women were known for their expertise at that very traditional dish.

Accidental Anthropologists

We had a lot of snow during that time, which meant Hilario was unable to make burrito deliveries. With snow piled up on the mesa, the Burrito Man couldn't get out to the road. I wanted to return the *sopa* container, so I set it on a little table in the enclosed front porch. It would catch my eye the next time Hilario appeared. Eventually, the deliveryman was able to make it out to the road and his route of customers.

I was always happy to see Hilario after what seemed like a long time, especially during winter. When he finally showed up, I grabbed the *sopa* container on my way out the door. I said, "Hilario, please tell Elvira how much we enjoyed the *sopa*. It was the best we have ever tasted. The almonds were the perfect touch."

He kind of snorted as he replied, "Hey, I made that *sopa*, not Elvira. I told you before, I'm the cook in that house." For the most part, men in the area didn't cook. It was a cultural thing, especially in Hilario's age group. The men went out to work, while the women stayed home and took care of the house, the children and the grandchildren. The women did all the cooking. So then, I asked Hilario where he learned to cook, because he was very creative and innovative, especially with his burritos.

The man's response made me laugh, because it was so unexpected: "In prison, where else? I was one of the best cooks there." I never asked when or why, for it didn't matter to me. What did matter was the fact that Hilario worked hard at making a living. He was proud of his product, and he had a right to be.

That Christmas season, Thomas and I spent a month in California. It was the first time we had been away from home for such an extended period. The weather was mild due to La Niña and especially dry. We arrived home on the Saturday after New Year's, and we both could have used a burrito that morning. It had been a long time since we had eaten one of Hilario's specialties.

When he hadn't shown up after a few days, we naturally assumed the man was suffering a huge hangover from all the holiday partying. However, by the end of the week, when he hadn't turned up, I began making inquiries. I always started at the post office, because Perfecto usually knew all the goings-on in the entire valley. Sure enough, Perfecto told me Hilario was in the hospital in Santa Teresa. I felt concerned, because Hilario's health was not good to begin with.

Perfecto went on to tell me that a few days earlier, Hilario had been drinking all day with the guys who were remodeling the state senator's place. At some point during the day, Hilario stumbled and tripped on a pile of debris. Because the man had both his hands in his pants pockets, he was unable to catch himself. The poor guy fell forward, cutting his face badly. Even worse, Hilario then reeled against a gas tank, breaking an arm and several ribs. The Burrito Man actually got himself up and to his car and then drove the long, winding road home to Hernandez Ranch. The thought of the injured man driving the washboard road with a broken body made me cringe. Perfecto told me an ambulance carried Hilario back down to the hospital in Santa Teresa, a fifty-mile drive. I hoped they gave him a lot of sedatives to ease his pain. More likely he had provided his own, earlier in the day.

When we learned of Hilario's story, Thomas said he would go by the hospital on Friday to check in on him. Then he was tied up with meetings and forgot. On Saturday morning, I called the hospital to see if he was still there. Perfecto and Pilar's daughter-in-law answered my phone call. Mary was a nurse, working the morning shift. When I told Mary of my concern for our friend, there was a long pause. Mary said very softly, "Oh Claudia, I am so sorry to tell you, Hilario passed away. He died last night. His injuries were much more severe than anyone realized."

Too many years of hard drinking had taken their toll. Elvira told me later, she never dreamed he would die, sober, in a hospital. Elvira had spent years worrying that Hilario would crash on one of the many sharp curves that drop off into oblivion, trying to find his way home from the valley below.

Hilario's death hit me hard, and I sobbed for the loss I felt. I couldn't imagine he would never drive up our road again, bringing with him that divine smell of red and green chile, not to mention the stories and characters that came along for the ride.

Hilario was so considerate of everyone. He was always thinking up ways to surprise his customers. One day he said to me, "You won't believe this, but when you told me you had never eaten Frito pie, I just had to make some for you." That was one of the few times I ever saw Hilario get out of his car. He opened the back door of the old Dodge, and there on the floor was a crock-pot filled with Texas chile. He had plastic bowls and spoons, and little bags of Frito chips, which he dumped into the bowl. He covered the chips with chile, chopped onions and grated cheese.

As he handed me the bowl, he said, "Today, I am proud to serve you Frito pie, fresh from Hernandez Ranch." At a dollar-fifty, Hilario was probably in the red. I was so touched and close to tears, all I could do was accept the bowl with gratefulness for his generosity. Hilario wouldn't back up (which is the way he always drove out our long, difficult driveway) until I had taken a few bites of his Frito pie. It was delicious, and he could tell by my face just how much I was going to enjoy his treat. I could hardly bear to think there would never be more of those treasures finding their way to our door.

Thomas took off work, and we drove up to Hernandez Ranch for Hilario's funeral the Monday after his death. We had never been up there, so the whole trip was one of amazement for us. Every now and again, on a curve, there was an open view of the Rocky Mountains away to the north. Against that background, Maxwell Mesa loomed up, huge and solid, as it curved away from us toward the west. With massive cloud formations and the valley stretching out below, it was no wonder Hilario loved driving up and down that road, day after day, rain or snow. Like other locals, the Burrito Man enjoyed the challenge of the elements.

We had to search for the Hernandez Ranch church, because you didn't see it from the main road into the village. We followed a car with Texas plates to the church, where there were already dozens of cars parked along the road. The church was quite small, and fortunately, there was just enough space for us in a back corner under the choir loft. By then, many people were already standing. As more and more friends and relatives arrived, they lined up along the wide walk in front of the church. It was a cold and cloudy day, with wind strong enough to make standing outdoors uncomfortable. However, valley folks were so hardy, standing outdoors in the wind never kept anyone from attending the funeral of a loved one.

I was happy we were able to get inside, because Hilario was lying in an open casket, and I hadn't realized how much I needed to see him for the last time. I was surprised at how dark Hilario's skin appeared next to the blinding whiteness of the casket lining.

Accidental Anthropologists

Loved ones got out of their pews to go stand next to Hilario in his casket. Some touched his face, and a few kissed his cheek for the last time. Thomas and I had never been to such a funeral. A funeral where people got up and wandered around, always tethered to the lovely wooden box. It was a homemade casket, lovingly made. Somebody had painted it a pale turquoise color and lined it with white satin fabric, done in just the right way. Hilario in his casket was the center of attention, and no one seemed in a hurry. It took quite awhile for the Mass to begin, because more and more people kept arriving.

Finally, at the end of Mass, people were encouraged to stand and say a few words about their relationship with Hilario. His childhood friends spoke of their time together, and then, one by one; children from previous marriages began to rise. The siblings spoke from their hearts of the father they had rarely seen over the years. A tall young man stood slowly and began to speak in a soft voice. He was the unknown son, unknown to all but Elvira and Hilario.

The young man said he was so relieved and happy to be called in time to spend a little time with his father before he died. Another son, who had been raised by Elvira and Hilario, got up to talk about the illness they shared, the illness of alcohol. Thomas and I were surprised at how comfortably everyone spoke about the terrible disease that killed our friend. I thought part of the reason we loved the culture so much, came from the fact that our neighbors accepted all the parts of their lives, good or bad. One did not necessarily make the other better or worse. It was all part of life in the land of enchantment.

Exactly one week after Hilario's funeral, Pilar and I drove up the winding road to Hernandez Ranch. We had decided to visit Elvira in order to take her a few things.

Claudia Clavel

I had a Christmas cactus called "Firecracker" because of the elongated, bright red flowers that bloom around Christmas time, which I had started from a plant that seemed on the edge of demise. I wanted to take a now-healthy specimen to Elvira, because she and Hilario used to admire my plants that spent the warmer months on the glassed-in front porch. When they drove up to our kitchen door, they were literally parked in front of what, to them, must have seemed like a greenhouse. Hilario had remarked more than once that he would like to have starts from any of my blooming plants.

Fortunately, I had started several sets of leaves from the cactus, and they all took root. I not only had a new plant for Elvira, but one for Perfecto and Pilar and myself. When I gave Elvira the cactus, I told her we would all have plants blooming at the same time, and it would be our collective reminder of Hilario. I also decided to plant a group of narcissus bulbs in the flowerbed next to the porch door as a yearly remembrance of Hilario's trips up our driveway. The flowers would bloom in front of where Hilario used to park his car and rev the engine.

When Elvira opened the door and invited us in, I was surprised to see her wearing an oxygen breathing tube. The long plastic tubing snaked its way all over the living room. I was afraid someone was going to step on it, cutting off her supply of air. Elvira laughed when I told her of my fear, but she said it wouldn't matter even if someone did. As the afternoon wore on, a number of people filtered in and out of the house. Surprisingly, no one ever did step on that tubing.

Elvira was short of stature and quite heavyset. The only other times I had seen her were in the car with Hilario, so it was good to see her up and around, in spite of the oxygen tube. Elvira was quite composed, and as I remarked on that, she said that she had been living with the fear of Hilario's death for a long time. It gave her comfort, knowing Hilario had gone to a better place. She knew that one day they would be together again. A given, in the Hispanic Catholic culture. Pilar handed her gifts to Elvira: a box of thank-you cards and fifteen dollars for candles at Masses in memory of her husband.

Elvira lived in a compound of mobile homes, just off the gravel road on the outskirts of Hernandez Ranch. As we sat, sipping warm Coca Cola, she told us how she and Hilario had met as children. They were born in Hernandez Ranch and lived across the road from one another. Elvira said she had always loved Hilario from the earliest time she could remember. She found every excuse imaginable to get his attention throughout their childhoods, but Hilario left the Ranch as a young man, seeking adventure in the big world below. The widow told us he was never moved by her ardent love for him.

Hilario moved away to Roswell to seek his fortune. There he married a number of times and had a series of children, in and out of wedlock. The man eventually returned to Hernandez Ranch in his fifties to live out the remainder of his life. By the time of his return, Elvira had been divorced. She was living on her own in the small compound of five mobile homes, most of them occupied by women and children. She pointed out to Pilar and me, the women in the compound had lost their men to some type of violent, alcohol-related death throughout the years she lived there.

Just then, a school bus pulled into the compound, unloading a group of children. Two of them ran up the porch steps and into the living room, where we women still sat exchanging stories about Hilario. Elvira introduced us to the girls, who were related to her: one a niece and the other a granddaughter. Miranda, the oldest, was fifteen and in high school. Venus, the younger girl, was ten and in fifth grade.

The girls were full of chatter and laughter, relating their school day to us. Pilar and I were surprised by how vivacious and outgoing they both were. Miranda said to me, "Oh, you're the lady who owned the Subaru Hilario bought last year?" It was the only four-wheel drive car with a horn that Hilario had ever owned. He bought it from us shortly before his death. I nodded as she went on, "You left a couple of tapes in the car, and we play them all the time. I never heard classical music before, and I love listening to them."

We had a great chat about the connection between classical music and math. I wasn't surprised to learn that math was her best subject. I promised to make more tapes for them to enjoy. Elvira said the girls would be living with her for quite a while, so there would be plenty of time for my efforts.

We could feel the winter sun sinking lower into the afternoon and realized it was time to head down the mesa toward home. The three of us women walked out onto the front porch, where we hugged and said goodbye. As I was backing the car around, each trailer in the compound came into my line of vision. I had to choke back a sob, thinking about Elvira and those girls, the latest in the long line of women to lose their men to a tragic death.

23

Libradita and Victoria's Secrets

It was with great sadness that I learned of the death of Libradita Torres, one of the liveliest of the San Ignacio inhabitants. She spent the last few years of her life in a nursing home in the little city of Santa Teresa. Before entering that facility, Libradita had lived her entire life on a dirt road at the back of the village, next door to her son, Procopio, and his family.

Libradita was a tiny woman, barely five feet tall. She weighed less than a hundred pounds and had the energy of a hummingbird. She fairly flew around the village during her active phase, which was pretty much spring and summer. By winter, Libradita had retreated inside herself and spent most of her time in a semi-reclusive state. The woman celebrated her 70th birthday climbing plum trees and delivering bagsful of plums to many of her neighbors. She was known throughout San Ignacio for her generosity and gift giving.

She was also known for her "sticky" fingers. Libradita had a penchant for kleptomania that bordered on the hilarious. Whatever she took, she gave to someone else, somewhere in the valley. I had my own experience with Libradita and her sleight-of-hand dexterity, when she lifted one of my, just-out-of-the-oven loaves of bread, apparently, when I turned my back for a moment.

Claudia Clavel

It wasn't until the next day, when I received a phone call from Pilar asking if I was missing a loaf of bread that I realized what had happened. I always baked five loaves of very heavy, whole-grain bread every two weeks and bagged four of them for the freezer. Pilar told me that Libradita brought my loaf of bread to her, saying, "*Hijolo*, that bread was too heavy for me. I could hardly cut it, but I didn't want to waste it so I brought it to you."

Pilar told me she recognized my bread because I was the only one in San Ignacio who would bake something like that. With no tact whatsoever, she informed me that my bread was too heavy for her and Perfecto. She took the loaf to Dulcinea to feed to her chickens. We had a good laugh over the thief and her generosity. The next time I walked by Dulcinea's house, I chuckled at the thought of her chickens feasting on my heavy bread.

A few weeks later Pilar phoned me, laughing heartily. She said, "You won't believe what just happened to me." I asked, and she continued, "Robin Hood struck again." Pilar told me Libradita had stopped by earlier for a visit, just as she was folding laundry. She had a stack of seven new dishtowels she had just finished embroidering. Each one had a colorful day of the week sewn into a corner. The towels were in a neat pile on the corner of her dining table. Pilar stopped to share a cup of coffee with her guest, and they were sitting at the same table.

With all her hummingbird energy, Libradita never stayed long in one place. Pilar's daughter, Christalina, mentioned that as Libradita was heading out the door, she looked like she had gained weight. It wasn't until Pilar went to put the laundry away that she realized her towels had gone missing. Christalina laughed, as she and her mother pondered who might be the recipient of Pilar's recent handiwork. I marveled at their good humor.

Accidental Anthropologists

It wasn't long before Christalina stopped laughing. The young woman was about twenty at the time, a very slim, athletic runner. She was attending college, working toward a degree in nutrition. Christalina was a "nose to the grindstone" type. However, she had a penchant for expensive Victoria's Secret lingerie and had recently received some as a gift. The young woman wouldn't allow her mom to wash her panties and bras in the washing machine. Christalina took great pains to wash her undies by hand in baby detergent, and then hang them on the clothesline to dry.

A week or so after the dishtowel caper, I received another phone call from Pilar, and she wasn't laughing. Christalina had come home from school and noticed her lingerie wasn't on the clothesline. She assumed her mom had taken them in for her. When Pilar informed her daughter that she had not even seen the bras and panties on the line, they knew. Robin Hood had made another strike.

Christalina was livid. But at dinner that night, Pilar reminded her daughter that Victoria's Secrets had been a gift, so she wasn't actually out any money. By then, Christalina and her family were able to have another laugh. And they wondered whether 75-year-old Libradita was wearing those frilly undergarments, or who else in the valley might have been trying to fit into them.

The last Robin Hood incident occurred shortly before Libradita went to live in the nursing home in Santa Teresa. Pilar received a phone call from a friend in another village, asking whether she was missing some jewelry. The caller said Libradita brought a necklace and some earrings to her as a gift, and the woman thought she had seen them on Pilar.

Claudia Clavel

My friend got in her car and drove to the caller's house for a jewelry inspection. They turned out to belong to someone else, but the two women were neither angry nor surprised. They understood Libradita suffered an illness. And they wouldn't blame her for that. In fact, they wound up laughing over to whom the jewelry might belong. And whether one of them should wear the jewels to church in order to attract the attention of the rightful owner.

24

Victoria, A Notorious Woman

I met Victoria in the waiting room of a doctor's office and felt sorry for her immediately. She was a waif-like woman, and appeared to be in her mid-forties, attractive in spite of two missing front teeth. The woman seemed so vulnerable I knew it was my fate to help her. We had a long wait and struck up a conversation about life in New Mexico. I learned a long-time live-in boyfriend had recently abandoned Victoria. She was in the process of having to move out of his house, which was in escrow. He gave the woman all the furniture, a four-wheel-drive vehicle, and no money whatsoever. She was looking for a cheap rental, and, unfortunately, I knew of one in the village. That was how our troubles began. I say our, because it ultimately involved the whole village.

Victoria began her move a few days after our meeting. I had introduced her to the landlord of a sweet little adobe on the plaza, and they agreed on the terms. I was astounded by the endless U-Haul trips that went on for a few days. Victoria had so much stuff, she had to ask the property owner for a garage ruin across the road, where she stored the overflow. By then, I was starting to have second thoughts about my offer to help her find a house to rent, especially as there seemed to be a line of slow-moving cars driving back and forth on that little-used dirt road. Some of the drivers were stopping to chat with the child-like woman, who was often in her backyard pondering garden plots or something unseen.

It didn't take long for the word to get around: a new, single woman had moved into the village. I decided I should have a talk with Victoria about village protocol and how important it was for her never to flirt with the men in the area. If she did, she would have to contend with the wives and in some cases that could be worse than fending off the Drinkers. "In other words," I told her, "just keep a low profile, mind your own business, and you should have a comfortable, simple life here." Victoria smiled at all the information, and I knew from that smile that San Ignacio would never be the same.

My studio window looked out on the little dirt road with a view of Victoria's backyard, and it was there that I became witness to the "vamping." Once she had her belongings assembled, Victoria found things to do in her backyard that required a lot of standing around. When she heard a car coming, she would step out onto the road and hold her hands together, like a frame. She would be looking through it, like a movie director working out a scene.

As the car approached, Victoria would step lightly into the yard, give a little wave, and resume her peering mode. The car would move on a ways and then back up slowly, coming to a stop next to where the woman was standing. Victoria and the driver would chat a while, and then he would drive on. Sometime later, the car would return, the driver would park in her yard, and some chore would be undertaken. I likened the behavior to fishing. Victoria would throw herself out into the road as bait and wait for a fisherman to pass by and cast his line.

Accidental Anthropologists

The woman would bite and let herself be reeled in. The guy didn't even need a net.

One by one, at the post office or buying eggs, the women asked me questions about our new neighbor. I felt guilty and embarrassed for leading her there, and it kept getting worse, day after day. Victoria had begun to bring little gifts to me, timed just as Thomas returned from work. He didn't seem to notice when Victoria fluttered her eyelashes at him, but the invitation was there. During one of her visits, I decided to speak to her about the women of the village and their uneasiness with the steady stream of men on the back road. With help from all those adoring fishermen, Victoria was turning that little adobe into her dream cottage. Her response to my concern was to become very indignant, first with the women and then with me for daring to utter the words.

Fortunately, Victoria would go off periodically to visit some guy in Utah and do whatever it was she had to do to get money from him. She told me that he was an old high school friend who came to her rescue financially when her former boyfriend dumped her. When she returned from one of those trips, she became obsessed with a project regarding the village. The church at that time was being refurbished on the outside, with local men doing all the work of removing old plaster and stabilizing the ancient adobe bricks beneath. It took a few summer months for them to re-plaster and paint the undulating walls.

Victoria became delirious with ambition to document the church restoration. And she did, day after day, dressed in her waif outfit of black leggings and an over-size man's white shirt with the sleeves rolled up. With camera in hand, the woman photographed the entire process from every angle. Each day, it didn't take long before all the workers were gathered together, passing out beer for a well-deserved break. Victoria was usually at the center of the group, a beer in hand. By then, you could see curtains moving ever so slightly, all around the village plaza, as Victoria moved around the group of workers.

The woman confided in me that she had been in contact with historical preservation people in Washington, D.C. She wanted to save San Ignacio for posterity. One hot summer day when we met, Victoria nearly shouted, "These people here have no idea what they have. This is beyond them. San Ignacio belongs to the world. It should be turned into a monument and tourist attraction." I stammered something about people having roots that went back hundreds of years and not wanting outsiders rolling through in their SUVs with their cameras pointed at them. She just smiled that horrible smile that I now recognized as trouble.

By then, you could feel the uneasiness that gripped the village. We all had the jitters, in spite of the fact that the number of cars on the back road had begun to dwindle once Victoria got all her needs met. Then the men began to squabble over her as one by one, they drifted in to collect payment for their labors. Victoria played one against the other, insinuating that she had favorites. In reality, I did not think she ever slept with any of them. She was just a tease, and that was a dangerous thing in these parts.

The final incident came when things began heating up on yet another level. Victoria took in a bunch of semi-wild cats that belonged to neighbors, who she felt weren't feeding them properly. Village cats were expected to hunt for their meals, and indeed, that is what they did. It didn't take long for the woman to give up on the idea of domesticating a bunch of semi-wild cats. The cats began breaking things in her little cottage, so out they went. Worse than that, Victoria had offered a calico cat to a bookstore owner in Santa Teresa.

Sandra, the bookstore owner and an old friend of mine, called to say that she and her husband were coming to pick up the cat and wanted to stop by our place. I asked who gave her the cat, as there was only one calico cat in the village and it belonged to Lorenzo, Victoria's next-door neighbor. Sandra said the gift giver was our neighbor, Victoria. Hearing this, blood rushed to my face, and I fought back fury as I explained to Sandra that the cat didn't belong to Victoria. We both agreed the woman didn't have the right to give away someone else's cat.

It happened that Lorenzo and I met at the end of our driveway the next day. I asked him how he felt about having his calico cat given away to a woman in Santa Teresa. There was a long pause as he lifted his head and looked at me. He said, "You know, I've had that calico for several years. She's a really good mouser, and I like having her around. Why do you ask?" I told him what had taken place in town, and that I wanted to be sure how he felt. I told him not to worry, that calico cat wasn't going anywhere.

As I told the story to Thomas that evening, he sat listening and pondering for a long time. Finally, he said, "You know, that Victoria has really screwed up the ecology here in the village. We're having mice again, and it's because she started feeding all the neighborhood cats, and now they aren't hunting. In fact, I haven't seen them around at all."

So there we were: village tremors, squabbling fishermen, and the ecology screwed up. All because of that woman down the road. Something had to be done, but what? That evening, Thomas and I set off for a walk on the back road. Victoria was in her yard, and Lorenzo's young stepson, Pancho, was on the roof next door. The boy yelled down to us, "Thomas and Claudia, hi, I'm looking for the new kittens. The calico cat had them yesterday. Lorenzo said for me to look and see whether she might have had a calico kitten. He said you could give your friend in town one if she did."

At the word "calico," Victoria sprang forward. "Calico, what calico?" she snarled.

"The one you tried to give Sandra Adams," I hissed. "How dare you take all those cats in, and then tire of them, to the point of giving them away! They aren't yours to give."

"They aren't taken care of!" she screamed.

Thomas broke in, his face redder than I had ever seen it, veins bulging out on his forehead. "You've totally screwed up the ecology of this village, in more ways than one," he said, his voice rising.

As Thomas continued, now yelling at Victoria, I saw out of the corner of my left eye Pancho's mother, Fabie, carrying a folding aluminum chair from her back porch. Without saying a word, she simply sat down next to the wire fence separating their place from Victoria's. She had come to see what was happening. Then I looked up to see Pancho sitting with his legs hanging over the edge of the roof, totally engrossed in the goings-on below. I had never felt so humiliated.

There we were, screaming at the waif/woman. Words were unintelligible as we were all shouting at once. Fabie and Pancho leaned forward as Victoria tore into me. She was screaming at me about ruining her reputation. She accused me of going to all the neighbors with rumors about her. That really kicked me into high gear, as I yelled, "I told you what would happen if you messed with the

Accidental Anthropologists

men here. And I didn't gossip. You've done this to yourself."

It was over like a summer storm: a final thunderclap, and then silence. We all glared at one another, and Thomas and I retraced our steps back to the road. We continued our walk in silence, actually getting our breathing back under control. By the time, we reached the cemetery, we were laughing at our behavior. The whole scene had taken us by such surprise. We walked back slowly, each in our own thoughts. Mine were focused on how to get that woman out of San Ignacio. I needn't have worried about that, for things had already been set in motion.

I was so embarrassed by my behavior I couldn't even go for the mail for a few days. I knew by then that everybody in the village had heard about the "rumble" in Victoria's backyard. I couldn't talk to anyone about the incident. I had to let my embarrassment wear off, like a felt pen mark on my arm.

By the next week, different people began telling me about the unfortunate things that had been happening at Victoria's place. Somebody stole her fuse box, and things were missing from her yard. That was one of the ways problem people were dealt with in the valley. The harassment went on for a couple of weeks, and the next thing we knew, day after day Victoria was bringing in U-Haul trailers. Finally, there were no more trips. What a relief. You could feel it all over the village. It was like a collective sigh: The now-notorious woman was gone.

A few days later, I received a phone call from my neighbor Delfinia. She asked whether I was going for the mail. I assured her I would be down within the next fifteen minutes. She said she would meet me at the pump house. Delfinia was there when I arrived, holding a dozen eggs. She handed me the carton and said, "I just wanted you to have these."

Claudia Clavel

Then her sister-in-law, Rosina, joined us and handed me a small bag of peas from her garden. The three of us stood in the shade of the pump house, chatting about gardens, weather and kids. We never mentioned our departed neighbor, for that was not the way in their culture. The next day, Pilar brought her sister-in-law, who was visiting from California, to meet me. Pilar also brought me a cabbage from a friend's garden. One by one, the village women let me know where I stood in the community. It was about then that my embarrassment finally began to wear off.

25

Los Ojos

May was the month for graduations; it was also the month when the howling winds of spring usually diminished a bit. There would be one day in May when it was warm, really warm, and you knew the heat would stay for a while.

Graduation parties were usually the first festivities after the long Lenten season and Easter, so they were anticipated with eagerness. Before the community center was built, most warm weather celebrations took place outdoors, even if the wind was blowing.

Thomas and I were invited to a high school gradu ation party for the daughter of Rosina and Claudio Archuleta on a Saturday afternoon. Maria and her family lived on the east side of the village, on a little dirt road down by the river. The party would be held in their drive-way, between their house and the property of Ambrosio Lovato, with whom they didn't get along. A chain-link fence separated the two properties, and blankets were thrown over the fence to create a windbreak and provide shade as the sun moved further to the west later in the day. Chairs and benches were lined up along the fence fac-ing the driveway, which would soon become a dirt dance floor.

Claudia Clavel

A long roof covered the *portal*, where the buffet table stood, laden with food. Party food was traditional, no matter the occasion: red chile with beef, green chile stew with pork and potatoes. There were pinto beans, the local staple, along with a cold cut platter and plenty of white bread. Jars of mustard and mayonnaise were available, in case you wanted a sandwich to dip into your chile of choice. You could count on enchiladas, a macaroni casserole, and potato salad. There was a green iceberg lettuce salad with chopped tomatoes and sliced radishes and an assortment of bottled salad dressings. Everyone seemed to love the fruit salad, mixed with Cool Whip. Red fruit punch was another staple. A large, traditional sheet cake, frosted with school colors and decorated for the occasion, rounded out the meal.

A couple of big ice chests sat at the front of the *portal*, one containing beer and the other an assortment of sodas on ice. Throughout the day, everyone helped themselves to food and drink. It had been announced that "jungle juice" would be served: a concoction of fruit juice and pure grain alcohol. Drinking jungle juice at high altitude during the heat of the day could be a lethal combination, and we knew where that might lead. Thomas and I had agreed beforehand to leave the party when the first glass of jungle juice was spilled, and that would not take long, as it turned out to be quite a hot day.

A small local band was providing music for dancing, and that was a special treat, for people in the valley loved to dance. Marcos and Graciela Pacheco were known throughout the valley for their traditional Spanish two-step and modern dance music. The New Mexico two-step could be very stylized, depending on village location. Thomas and I had once attended a dance in the high mountain village of Chula Vista where the two-step was

Accidental Anthropologists

so choreographed you could pick out family members, from young to old, who had been trained in their particular style. It was much the same with chile recipes; each village had its distinctive version.

Thomas and I had always enjoyed village parties. It was the one time we could sit with our neighbors, catch up on family gossip and notice how the children had grown since our last encounter. We arrived at the party early for a change, as we usually kept working right up to the last moment before any event. We knew there would be a lot of drinking as the afternoon wore on, so for us, early was the best choice. The children were in high spirits, with the band belting out their favorite Spanish songs. Every now and then, one of the little girls would twirl out into the dance space and move to the music. The teenagers and little boys would never have done that. They were much too shy for dancing in front of their parents. None of the adults were dancing yet; that usually came later, after everyone had a few drinks to loosen up.

Thomas was off to one side, drinking beer with the men. As it was May, they were talking about planting and the traditional *acequia* system that delivered irrigation water to all the small fields in the valley. For over one hundred fifty years, every village in northern New Mexico had had an *acequia* ditch that provided enough water to grow their chile, corn and beans. In early spring, all the men in the villages would be out with their hoes, cleaning weeds and grass out of the ditches. Then they burned whatever was growing along the banks. When we saw smoke during that time, we knew spring had arrived.

I sat with the women in the shade, chatting sporadically and enjoyed the fact that we didn't have to have continuous conversation in order to spend time together. It was pleasant enough just to sit, watching the children and listening to the music. Occasionally, to everyone's delight and amusement, Marcos and Graciela's eleven-year old daughter, Destiny, would grab the microphone and sing a few songs in Spanish. The guests clapped and shouted out requests. They loved to see their traditions carried on by the children.

Out of nowhere, a huge gust of wind came up, and as it picked up speed, it began to swirl into a mini-tornado. The dirt dance floor began flying in every direction as we all raced to the *portal*. Our hosts were quickly covering food and trying to keep the paper plates from soaring off to Texas. In front of our eyes, the sky turned black over the mesa, and then big, fat raindrops began to pelt the ground. It all happened so quickly, we couldn't figure out exactly what to do, so the whole party just stood, crammed together around the food table, waiting for it to let up.

Then there was a shriek. Angela, a guest and noto-rious flirt from another village, had spilled her glass of jungle juice. She was weaving a bit and unsteady on her feet. Her outburst seemed to break the spell the wind had on us. Thomas and I looked at one another across the *portal* and smiled. We had our signal. We moved toward our hosts, thanked them, congratulated the graduate and said goodbye to our neighbors.

All our windows were open at the house; so we braced ourselves for the cold raindrops, ducked our heads and ran all the way home in a headwind. By the time we reached our place, the storm was over as quickly as it had begun. It had been a wonderful party for us, with just the right amount of time.

Two weeks later, Delfinia phoned me to ask about planting something. We chatted for a bit, and finally she asked, "You haven't heard about what happened at the party after you and Thomas left?"

Accidental Anthropologists

"No," I replied.

"Well," Delfinia went on, "you know how much Angela bugs me, don't you?"

"Yes," I replied, "you've made that pretty clear. What happened?"

Delfinia continued, "Angela was getting pretty drunk on that jungle juice. You saw her spill her drink just before you left. Then we all started dancing, and Angela kept cutting in on the women. By then, she was after all of the men on the dance floor. I got madder and madder, and told my Palemon, 'Don't you dare dance with that woman.' Then I sat down for a while, and the more I watched Angela, the more my blood boiled."

Delfinia paused a moment, taking a deep breath, and then she went on, "The next thing I knew, she was asking my Palemon to dance. That did it. I jumped up and went over to her, and I can't believe what I said to her; I said, 'You, *pinche pendejo*' in a real loud voice. 'I saw you give my Palemon *los ojos* (the eyes).' Claudia, you could have heard a pin drop. Nobody said nothing. They just sat there with their mouths open. I couldn't believe I did it, but this had been building up in me for a long time."

Delfinia took another breath, and then went on, "I just turned away and walked back to my chair. The band played another song, but nobody danced for a while."

Stunned, I sat for a moment. Delfinia was a rather quiet woman, usually keeping her thoughts to herself, though she had confided in me a few times about her feelings toward the flirt, Angela. Finally, I said, "Delfinia, you probably did all those women a big favor by telling Angela to keep her hands off the men here. I doubt she will ever try that again around you. Good for you. Now it's out of your system and you can relax."

Claudia Clavel

Delfinia's response to me was this: "So, Claudia, you and I are watching out for the men of San Ignacio. We're not going to let no outside women come in here and mess with our men, right?" After the Victoria incident, I had to agree with her.

26

San Ignacio and the Movie Business

Movie companies found San Ignacio around 1984, when a scene for "Young Guns" was shot in the village. That was the year before we moved there, but the story was still being told: "Young Guns" met the village wild bunch. It was never determined who made the deal with the film company or how the money was distributed. It was said that nobody in the village made any money from that movie, but a couple of people bought new pickup trucks, so they were suspects. In reality, shooting one scene for a film would not pay enough to buy two new vehicles. However, the locals weren't aware of that, so rumors were flying. A lot of hostility was being played out among the disgruntled men, and our neighbor, Sixto aka Comanche was at the head of the list. The two of us were about to become better acquainted.

The day of the movie shoot, the film crew drove through a gauntlet of locals and non-locals who were holding picket signs that read: "We Work For $$" and "Outsiders Not Welcome." To make matters worse, some of the guys began playing loud music on their car radios and endlessly honking their horns. The sheriff had to be called, but not before threats began flying. The movie people were furious for the expensive delays, and the locals were furious because they had not been part of the plan.

Claudia Clavel

Eventually, this controversy led to Thomas and Marcos Pacheco becoming the liaison team to work with the New Mexico Film Office, the movie companies and the village of San Ignacio. With all the dissension over shooting movies there, someone in the village had to be responsive to all parties.

However, this didn't happen until after an incident occurred at the bottom of our driveway shortly after we moved in. Thomas was fixing coffee at dawn one summer morning when he looked out our kitchen window and saw a little old man wearing a serape and a broad-brimmed straw hat. The man was playing a little concertina on the dirt road down below our driveway. As he played, the bow-legged man danced next to Lorenzo's old outhouse. Behind him, a red-orange sunrise broke over the mesa to the east, creating a magnificent backdrop. Then the dancer disappeared. My husband could hardly believe what he was witnessing, until he saw the little old man dance back onto the road again, still playing his concertina.

Right then, our California houseguest passed by the window, heading down the driveway toward the action. Thomas quickly joined Howie, and then saw a film crew around the corner of the stone house below us. The two men soon learned that the crew was shooting an opening scene for "The Milagro Beanfield War." Thomas woke me and ran to fetch Howie's wife, Berta, so we could watch the scene being shot. Thomas also learned that no one in the village knew how the film crew came to be there.

"Natural Born Killers" was the next film that Hollywood wanted to shoot in San Ignacio. This time, before any agreements were signed, a village meeting was called to choose a film team. Thomas and Marcos were elected. The filmmakers wanted to shoot a car chase

Accidental Anthropologists

scene, starring Woody Harrelson. We all became excited over that prospect but were sorely disappointed to learn that car chase scenes are often shot in slow motion and then speeded up in the editing process. With such a small crew and only one star, we hardly noticed much action at all, except for watching Feliciano drag his dead mare through the movie set. The thrill for Thomas came when Oliver Stone drove up our driveway to hand over a check for fifteen hundred dollars. The money was divided between the village water association and the community center, so for the first time the movie business made nearly everyone happy.

The next film was "Speechless," starring Michael Keaton and Geena Davis. I was urged by the casting director to recruit our shy neighbors into working as extras for a one-day shoot. It took some convincing, but once folks realized they would be paid fifty-five dollars a day plus meals and would be part of a large crowd, just standing around, the idea became more acceptable.

The casting company hired two hundred valley locals to play a rowdy crowd scene during a political rally. They knew they had picked the right locale when a couple of guys in the back row started shoving each other over something known only to them. Thomas and I were part of the crowd of extras, and we worked on being rowdy for ten hours. Toward the end, the director was making progress, primarily because there were only two Porta Potties for a crowd of two hundred. Thomas quipped that line dancing must have originated then and there.

Thomas turned out to be very comfortable in his role as an extra actor and was approached for other scenes, but because he worked full time, he had to turn them down. Everyone in the village had a great time being a part of moviemaking. Best of all, we hardly had to leave our homes to get to work. The village agreed it was a great way to make money for the community. It was a clean industry that brought a little excitement and glamour to our humble corner of the world, for just long enough. The next movie would not be as easy.

From the beginning, "The Hi-Lo Country" was different. For one thing, the entire crew had agreed to work at reduced salaries in order to accommodate Max Evans, an Albuquerque author in his early seventies who had been trying for thirty years to get his book made into a movie. The author was afraid he would die of old age before that happened. Stephen Frears, a British director with PolyGram Filmed Entertainment, had been given the "The Hi-Lo Country" book by Martin Scorsese, who urged the director to turn it into a film. When we met, Frears told me he had always wanted to make a Western movie, and Evans' story captivated him at just the right time in his career.

The film company's location manager was always the first person to make contact with the community liaison people, and on that occasion, David Foster contacted me. By then, Thomas had begun working in town and was no longer available. Marcos had already changed his mind about his role as co-liaison. The State Film Office then asked me to take on the role. David told me about the film crew wanting to help immortalize Max Evans and get his movie made. He asked if I would help him out by asking the community to take a bit less for the four-day shoot of a fiesta scene.

By that time, I knew people of the village fairly well and told David Foster that most of my neighbors had no interest in the art of movie making and less interest in being immortalized. Besides, four days of film disruption

Accidental Anthropologists

was a huge issue for the community. One day was a major inconvenience. Four days would be a pain in the butt.

I did add that as an artist I would be willing to stand before my neighbors and try to impress on them the value of supporting the concept of creating a fine piece of art with very little money. Besides, I, too, personally wanted to help Max Evans get his book made into a serious movie. We had met during the first scouting event, and I learned he had been in and out of San Ignacio since he was a kid, working as a cowboy up on the mesa. Max told me that he retained a romantic nostalgia for the village because of the friendly folks he had met nearly sixty years earlier.

Meanwhile, David Foster dropped by on a regular basis, as he began putting together a plan for the exact location of the fiesta scene. There was a point when I realized David thought I had so much influence within the village that I could just tell my neighbors what they should do or accept. Nothing could have been further from the truth.

By then, we were sparring around the issue of money. In the past, the village had negotiated for one thousand dollars a day for a movie shoot. I didn't think they would take less than that. It just wasn't worth it to them for the hassles involved. Thomas and I wrote a letter to the community, telling them about Max Evans and the movie crew working for reduced wages in order to get the movie made. We called for a gathering in front of the church, and I read the letter to the crowd. Our neighbors looked straight through me, as if they had not heard a word I said.

Then the rumors began. The next morning, Marcos came by to tell me there was a rumor that he, Thomas and I were on the take from PolyGram Filmed Entertainment.

185

Claudia Clavel

The madness had begun. Two days later, a young woman drove up to our house to tell me she had been sent by a friend who wanted to know whether Thomas and I had been on the take from the last movie, because we had gone to Europe the summer before. Her friend wanted her to see my face when she asked, so she could determine whether I was lying. I kept my composure and assured the young woman we had definitely not received any favors from the film company. Thomas and I were devastated by the rumors, especially as we had been respected in the community and were aware of how quickly alliances can shift.

Thomas had been turning out weekly movie notices, informing folks of everything that was taking place with the film company and always reminding the community of working together for the good of all. The rumors persisted. I was proud of Thomas's levelheaded approach and the way he maintained a positive attitude. For me, I simply wanted to burn everyone's house to the ground in order to stop the negative vibes that had taken over the entire village.

The usual response from the object of a local rumor was to be quiet and hope it would soon pass. It had always worked that way in the valley. However, it didn't work for me. I began to get sick to my stomach, and I wanted to divorce the village and all those included. I begged Thomas to sell our place immediately and get me away from the madness. When he calmly refused, that kicked me into action. The next day, I began to rant. When I went for the mail, I ranted to the postmaster and whoever else might be in the building. I raved on and on about truth and honesty, volunteerism and community.

I saw Lorenzo drive his red and white activity bus into the plaza and park in front of Roque's house. I marched down to the bus, climbed on, greeted the four or five Drinkers sitting in the lined-up seats, and then launched into my monologue about rumors, truth and honesty. The men sat and listened politely as I ranted on. I asked about their families and left, feeling somewhat vindicated.

I spent the next week dropping in on my neighbors for the sole purpose of delivering my speech. My face often turned red from indignation as I delivered the same words, over and over. The people of the village were much too polite to interrupt when someone was speaking, so I had the floor to myself. I would never know whether the entire community was laughing at me or sitting in disbelief as I ranted on. However, I didn't care. No way was I just going to sit up on that hill and allow the rumors to continue. I was sixty-two years old and tired of a whole lot of stuff. I could feel myself filling up with some kind of force that was propelling me forward.

Shortly after my speech rounds, I went for the mail. There were three men inside the post office. As I opened my box, Roque stepped toward me and began to rant at me. He said that I was on his enemy list. My heart froze as the other two men darted out the door, and Perfecto stepped behind the mailboxes. At that time, Roque was a hopeless drunk, and he could be mean. My ears began to buzz as I heard him say, "You didn't pay attention to me on the bus. You ignored me like I wasn't there." He went on, "Nobody, I mean nobody from that movie company better come near my property, or I'll shoot every one of them." In that moment, the whole thing became very scary.

Meanwhile, the movie company was in and out of the village for one reason or another. The Monday after the post office incident, I happened to be on my way to pick up the mail, and before I entered the plaza, I stopped in my tracks. I saw movie people scattered throughout the plaza and then noticed David heading toward Roque's house. I started to shout, "Get back," but it was too late. Roque was approaching the location manager. I held my breath for an instant, but David was already walking away. He told me later that Roque had threatened him and the rest of the crew if they came near his house.

To complicate my life even more, the art director phoned, asking whether I might know of a building where they could store some scenery. It needed to be secure. Without thinking, I offered my studio, which was unused at the time. I also offered our yard for their picnic tables and crudely made booths for the fiesta scene. What the art director neglected to tell me was the fact that there would be a security guard posted in front of our driveway for three days and nights. Just what we didn't need: more attention on us, where even the slightest change could throw people off balance. To make matters worse, I was asked to help find a local security guard. It had to be someone who could be trusted and was experienced. That really narrowed it down.

Magically, at that very moment, our neighbor Tito Garcia drove up and honked his horn. He had heard the film company was looking for just the qualities he possessed. We didn't know he had that background and were thrilled for Tito, as he, like everyone else in the village, always needed money. He filled out the paperwork on our kitchen table and said he was to begin that same night.

Later that evening, Thomas and I went to town for groceries and dinner out. On our way home, we stopped at La Tienda to pick up a movie. We bumped into the "Hi-Lo" security guy in the store, and he said something about

Accidental Anthropologists

his man being on the job at our place. When we got home, we saw Tito parked in our driveway near the house. Thomas and I got out and walked over to his truck. The new security guard was beaming, and we noticed a security badge pinned to his shirt. Tito would make some good money for three 12-hour shifts, so he was feeling good and especially proud. He said to us, "Thomas and Claudia, I want you to sleep well tonight, knowing I'll be out here, with my big old 45 to protect you." We saw the gun lying on the seat next to our guard and didn't know whether to laugh or cry.

I had to admit that Thomas and I did sleep like babes that night. My imagination had been running away with me, and for the first couple of nights after my run-in with Roque, I had been waiting for the smell of smoke as our house was being torched. That seems extreme now, but, in the past, the area had a reputation for some outrageous behavior. The next morning when Thomas went out for the paper, he saw a car parked at the bottom of our driveway. He walked down to see whom it belonged to just as the driver opened his door and stepped out. The man introduced himself and told Thomas he was the day security guard. As Thomas related the news to me, I began to shake. All I could think about were all those eyes staring up at us.

A couple of days later, the minute the guards were sent off somewhere else, I was out the door ranting once more. This time to the little general store owned and operated by our state senator neighbor, Isaac. It was the day before the movie shoot, and I became increasingly distraught over the possibility of what might happen when the film crew showed up. I felt I had one more chance to state my case, so I headed down to the senator's general store on the plaza.

Claudia Clavel

As I stepped through the door, I was so wound up, I didn't even say hello. I jumped right into my monologue about truth and honesty, not allowing Isaac to break eye contact with me. It was then I noticed that I was pounding on Isaac's counter, but I couldn't stop. The senator stood behind his counter in shock, finally saying, "If you hear one more rumor, you just come to me, and I'll take care of it." That didn't make me feel any better.

Then a side door opened, and in stepped Herculano, who worked for Isaac. The big, solid man stood tall, with his boots planted firmly on the floor. He looked directly at me and said in a deep voice, "Mrs. Clavel, you don't have to go to Isaac. I'm the meanest asshole in San Ignacio. If one more person comes to you with a rumor, I'll kick their ass."

Waving my hands in the air, I shouted, "Thank you! Thank you!" Then I remembered Roque. "What about Roque?" I shouted. "He's threatened to shoot any of the movie people if they go near his place!" Isaac jumped in, "Don't worry about Roque, I'll give him some money, and send him out of town."

At that, Herculano stepped forward. "No," he said. "I'll tie Roque up and take him out." I felt a flood of relief wash over my body. At last, somebody was ready to take action on my behalf. I wanted to hug Herculano, but I knew better. And suddenly it was over. Thomas said he could feel it too. He thought people wanted us to fight back and were relieved when we finally did. The experience had forced me to find my voice. It wouldn't be long before I would need it again.

The fiesta scene went extremely well. The plaza was festooned with strings of lights draped across the tops of the brightly painted, wooden streetlight structures. Picnic tables and benches were scattered throughout,

Accidental Anthropologists

along with metal tables and chairs. There were a watermelon booth, a tamale booth and another that sold serapes. Booths lined the plaza and attracted the extra families out for the evening festivities. We were seventy-five extras, dressed up in 1940s' clothing. We had our hair styled, cut or combed and had makeup applied lightly. We were considered "background," and our faces would not be in focus.

You could feel the excitement build as Stephen Frears waited for the perfect evening light. Meanwhile, the entire cast went over the scene, getting directions from the two assistant directors until we all knew our moves. Then Frears shouted, "Action!" and away we went as an ensemble. Thomas and I were told to walk across the plaza to a picnic table directly in front of Roque's house. I nearly balked, but Thomas pulled me forward. Then it dawned on me that a huge chunk of action was taking place not just in front of Roque's house but some of it on his front porch.

Thomas and I looked at one another with the same question on our minds. "Where was Roque? Had Isaac given him money and sent him out of town? Or had Herculano tied him up and taken him out?" There was no time to pursue those thoughts, as the director yelled, "Action!" again. I whispered to Thomas, "If Roque starts shooting, they should just keep the camera rolling."

We did the scene repeatedly, until about the eleventh "take", when we heard Stephen Frears say, "Great job." The director had made it all seem so easy to get people to do what he wanted. Thomas and I were beginning to enjoy the movie-making business, and we could tell that our neighbors had enjoyed it too. It was the talk of the village for quite a while, and even with all the hassles, we all looked forward to another movie experience.

Claudia Clavel

We never did know where Roque was during the shooting of the scene. However, he would turn up again in a major role when the next movie rolled into town the following year.

27

All the Pretty Horses Rode Into Town

On an unusually warm June afternoon, J.B. Smith, location manager for the New Mexico Film Office and my contact as liaison for the village, called me on his cell phone to say that he and a large group of location scouts for "All the Pretty Horses" were nearing San Ignacio.

J.B. and I had worked together before, so we both knew the routine: I would escort the group around the village, so they could photograph possible sites. They gave me an outline of the scene and what they were looking for specifically, and I walked them to a possible location. The art director, construction manager and film crew discussed the technical pros and cons at every stop. Sometimes we returned to the same site several times, until they were sure it would work. Charlie Harrington, the location manager for Columbia Pictures, told me they were looking for a site that could double as a Mexican village. There would be one scene, involving a jail.

As I was leading the group around the village, we had to pass Gilbert and Flora Salazar's place, and I was surprised to see their Doberman pacing along the inside of their fence line. The dog was growling and snarling, but usually village dogs never crossed their invisible territorial lines, so I wasn't too nervous, until the dog began to move toward the open driveway entrance. There were about nine people in the group. I was in the front and urged them to move on quickly, for the animal appeared intent on becoming a serious threat. Just as the last straggler passed by the driveway, the dog lunged at me.

Without thinking, I stepped forward instead of backward and snarled back at the dog, "Get back, and shut up." The Doberman seemed stunned for a moment, and that gave me time to move off slowly. The group had gathered a ways off and was watching me. The dog growled again, but by then, I knew he wouldn't come after me. Charlie said, "Man, I nearly wet myself. How could you remain so calm and back that dog down?" Shaking and laughing, I replied, "I was terrified but determined."

The next time I got the call from J.B., two vans and a private vehicle filled with film crew were already entering the village. I met them in front of Tito Garcia's house, where there was a little plaza-like area at the intersection of two dirt roads at the back of the village. Manuel Sanchez's back door would become the entrance to the jail in the scene. Two American prisoners, flanked by a group of Mexican soldiers, would be led on horseback along the dirt road to the Mexican jail scene. Tito's home played a big part in that scene, so he was making some good money, along with many of his neighbors along the back road.

I recognized some of the faces of the crew from our previous meeting, as Charlie took me by the arm and moved me toward the director, Billy Bob Thornton. The director thanked me for making their job easier and especially for introducing the crew to my neighbors. The large group moved around the area, each with a very different set of eyes. Some were creating sets and weighing technical possibilities, as others were assessing buildings around the little plaza and how they might fit into the scene. It was exciting standing among the crew, listening to people create an entire scene for a film that had not been shot yet. I loved the movie-making process on that creative level and was amazed when the crew spent no more than an hour making their decisions. It was a simultaneous agreement among those gathered to end the scouting session. Then a question arose.

Billy Bob Thornton asked where he might use a bathroom. Everyone looked around and saw no possibility, so I replied that he could use our bathroom. Somebody shouted, "We're going to Claudia's!" With that, everyone piled into vehicles, and we all drove to my house. I showed the director to the bathroom, saying I would be outside with the crew. When Thornton rejoined our group, he said, "I really like your home. And what was the red fabric piece hanging near the john?" I had to think a moment, but a guy in the group shouted that it was a *Mola*, an intricately cut-and-sewn art piece made by San Blas Indians off the coast of Panama. The crewmember said he had used our bathroom during their last trip. Then others chimed in that they had used it as well.

We all had a good laugh about the bathroom stop and shook hands until our next meeting.

Once the site was officially chosen, I had to call a village meeting, so there could be a vote on whether to rent our selves out again. At that gathering, I remembered "The Hi-Lo Country" fiasco, and realized I would be sticking my neck out again if I were to become involved. I said as much to the assembled group, but someone said, "Claudia, you have to do it. You're the only one who can pull it off."

I thought for a while, aware that I did love the movie-making process. Not to mention the fact that a lot of money was going to be pumped into our community. However, I reminded them that if there was any trouble, including rumors, I would dump it on the village, and they would have to be responsible.

To my surprise, my neighbors told me I could do anything I needed to do to make it work. That confidence set me free and propelled me forward. There was a vote to sign the long legal contract, and I reminded everyone again that movie companies do not play games once a contract is signed. It was serious business. And that would soon be tested.

When "All the Pretty Horses" rolled into town, with too many semis, star trailers, horse trailers, honey wagons and scenery, the entire village went into shock. The director wanted everyone packed into the village, because he thought we might all "bond." I had to demand that they leave enough room for cars to get to and from the post office, not to mention our homes.

From the beginning, people knew they would be compensated for their inconvenience, but Sixto wanted none of it. He was one of the original troublemakers who had caused upheaval during prior movie shoots. The man was on a mission to destroy the latest one that he thought had brazenly invaded our quiet little village.

The location manager and I connected immediately. We both knew what the other wanted and were capable of delivering it. I had not worked on that level for a very long time, but it stirred something dormant in me, and I felt that I was about to become really alive.

Momentum began to build as the construction crew rolled into the village to begin constructing set pieces. It was then I got my first call to arms. Charlie phoned to tell me that some guy, who called himself Comanche was threatening the crew. I had already had a run-in with Comanche the day after the village movie meeting. He tracked me down, and using his most menacing tone of voice, threatened to bring in a Hells Angels motorcycle gang to disrupt the filming. I told him to go ahead and make the call, for I thought Billy Bob Thornton could work it into the scene. Comanche was bluffing, of course, but that did not mean he was finished. The man was beginning to scare people, and that became my problem.

To further complicate my life, there was a death in the family of one of the production location guys, and Charlie came to me with news that he wanted to hire me to fill in for Len. All I could think about was "The Hi-Lo Country" rumor and how that had played out. The thought of being officially on the payroll of the movie company sent me reeling, and I begged Charlie to let go of the idea. He refused, explaining that I was key to the process because it all had to do with making sure tranquility prevailed during the few days of shooting. I was handed a walkie-talkie and told to report to work at seven a.m.

My first thought on the job was, "Why would anyone call me?" That's when I got the call from Charlie about Comanche.

However, before I could confront Comanche, the Columbia security manager found me and asked for help in hiring local security people for the three-week shoot. After some serious thought on the matter, I assembled my neighbors, and with their shocked blessing, I hired six of the Drinkers to work as security guards for the duration of the filming. My theory being, that it was that group which would cause trouble, especially if outsiders were hired. The security manager and Charlie agreed with my reasoning.

Because the Drinkers were sober at the time and relished making good money for a change, they became a happy and dedicated bunch. I told them, "If you drink during working hours, you will be fired on the spot." They didn't need to be told how serious their jobs were, or how much depended on their integrity. Each man shook my hand and thanked me for having confidence in him. Our neighbors looked on in disbelief, and I prayed, but felt they could do it. Then it was time to deal with Comanche.

Because I had faced the death threat the year before, and as a result had found my voice, I foolishly felt utterly fearless. Everyone knew about Comanche and his threats, so when I announced that I was going to confront him, the Drinker security guards gathered as a group, along with the location manager and a few other crewmembers. They were across the plaza from Comanche's house, standing around, watching me as I disappeared behind the troublemaker's *coyote* fence. My neighbor and I stood toe to toe, as I explained to him in a very controlled voice just what he was doing to the community with his bullying behavior. I also reminded him of how much he was disliked by his neighbors, and how much money was involved should they lose it because of him.

Comanche had been paid, like other neighbors, a hundred and fifty dollars for the use of his front yard for parked movie vehicles. I had been told that I could offer him an extra hundred dollars, a bribe to be sure, but a small price for the film company to get the scenes shot.

We talked a while, because I hoped to convince Comanche that he could really enjoy the movie experience if he would let go of his disruptive behavior. I urged him to consider being an extra, so he could participate in the process. He lit up at that prospect, and suddenly his demeanor shifted. The next thing I knew, the man dashed into one of his little adobe sheds and returned with a bag containing a frozen pork roast from a pig that had recently been butchered. I was completely surprised by his gift offering and as we walked to his gate, I nearly fell over when he gave me a big hug in front of the group of onlookers across the plaza. By then, I think we both knew that had things gone badly behind Comanche's *coyote* fence, there would have been another scene entirely.

28

Action!

With that problem behind us, we headed into the Electric Co-Op saga, which would test the entire production. The art director informed me that several electric lines had to be taken down on the back road where the major scene was to be shot. I phoned the manager of our Electric Co-Op, and he said the lines could be taken down. Then he added, "For a fee of five thousand dollars."

At that news, all hell broke loose on the set. The week before, in another scene, the same request had been met in Santa Teresa for a cost of a few hundred dollars. It was early on the day before the scene was to be shot, and everything depended on the lines being removed. The Electric Co-Op manager and I went round and round on the phone over cost, but he wouldn't budge.

By early afternoon, Columbia Pictures got involved, calling the State Film Office and then the governor's office. They were all yelling at the Electric Co-Op manager, who was then yelling at me about how much he hated the movie business. At the last possible moment, with a threat from the governor, the co-op manager said, "OK, here's the deal. Since you are a co-op member, the only way I'll take those lines down is if you personally write me a check for a six-hundred-dollar deposit and deliver it to the Alamos office." That was a twenty-mile drive in pouring rain, and I got there with minutes to spare before the office closed.

They faxed my check to the manager at the head office, and, just in time, a utility truck followed me back to the village, where they removed the electric lines. A cheer went up from the throng of people in the little plaza.

Early the next morning there was a knock on our door. It was Charlie, the location manager, with an envelope containing six hundred dollars. He said he was horrified that I personally had to pay for the electric lines to be taken down. We stood for a moment, reflecting on the bizarre series of events, and then shared a laugh about my having to cover Columbia Pictures' ass.

The big day had begun, and the cameras would soon be rolling. You could feel the excitement ripple through the village. A huge circus-type tent had been erected in the middle of the plaza where Billy Bob Thornton would host the entire village for a midday feast. I had gone door to door to get an official count for the food service folks, and all fifty-five households signed on. Little did we know they planned to serve filet mignon, among an array of dishes that some residents had never experienced in their lives.

I had to smile earlier that morning when I started my rounds and neared the breakfast food trailer. There were all the Drinker security guards standing in line, laughing with crewmembers as they waited for their custom-ordered omelets. Macario was even there with his toothless grin, and I could tell he was enjoying his role as village *coyote*. Charlie told me later that the crew was having a great time with all our colorful characters.

Accidental Anthropologists

Charlie put me right to work, doing the bidding of the art director. The first thing the man wanted was permission to put fake smoke in a woodstove in Amado's little stone *casita*. His house was just down the way from the *plazita*. As we walked toward Amado's, the director explained to me that on film, normal smoke does not show up. I knocked on the door, and we waited a while before ninety-three-year-old Amado greeted us. I introduced the art director and slowly explained what he had told me about fake smoke and what he wanted to do.

The *viejito* laughed heartily, shaking his head as he looked at us and said, "*Hijolo*, I have a lot of fire wood. You don't need no fake smoke." I told him the movie people would pay him fifty dollars if he would let them put the smoke container in his stove. The old man really laughed at that, as he replied, "OK, here's the key to my house. We're going to the senior citizens' lunch. You lock up and put the key under that rock when they finish smoking. But I could make a lot of smoke for them with my *piñon* wood."

Amado and his friend were still chuckling as they headed slowly toward the big plaza and their ride to lunch in the senior citizen van. The art director told me he loved that experience. He said it was one of the reasons he liked making movies on location.

As the momentum began to build for the big scene, Charlie sat on the Muñoz front *portal* smoking a cigarette while I ran my legs off. Finally, I went over to him and said, "Hey, why am I doing all your work while you sit there enjoying yourself?" He replied with a smile, "I want you to have the full film-making experience. I especially enjoyed watching you talk that old man into letting us put fake smoke up his chimney."

Claudia Clavel

I had to admit, I was having a great time. That is, until the close-up scene with Matt Damon and Lucas Black, the two American prisoners. They were riding horses up the dirt road to the Mexican jail, surrounded by all those Mexican soldiers. Out of camera range, there was a large group of people watching the filming, including Cormac McCarthy, author of "All the Pretty Horses."

My walkie-talkie buzzed, and it was the voice of one of the assistant directors. He sounded breathless as he said in a very serious tone, "Claudia, we have a situation here at the close-up location. A guy with a gun has just threatened to shoot all of us. You have to get him."

Because moviemaking is driven by adrenalin-fueled hyper-mania, the minute you step into that space, you automatically become a part of it. Without hesitation, I headed toward the scene and saw Roque Romero coming through an open space between two buildings. I could see the gun butt sticking out of his pants. Another location guy was on the back road, sort of herding Roque toward me. When the gun wielder saw me, he threw his hands up in the air, and in a singsong voice called out, "Hi Claudia, I'm not doing anything wrong." He was the same guy who had threatened all of us the year before during "The Hi-Lo Country" filming. And he was still a drunk.

As Roque came toward me, I reached out and grabbed him by his shirt collar. Pulling him toward me, I got in his face and snarled, "You have gone too far this time." All of a sudden, I felt a hand on my shoulder. It was Roque's gun-toting friend, turning me toward him. It was hard not to stare at the gun tucked in his waistband. In a nasty tone of voice, the guy hissed, "Hey, you don't mess with my friend."

"Back off," I snarled with such incredible fury that the guy did back away. I was still holding onto Roque, and he had turned into a child. Using that singsong voice, he said he and his friend would leave and stop causing trouble. Trying to control myself, I responded, "You'd better, because the police are on their way." That was not a lie, for someone had called earlier.

As Roque and his friend moved away from the area, I began shaking violently. My heart was racing, and I thought I might faint, but just then, the crew of two hundred began to applaud. Theresa, the casting director, ran toward me shouting, "Oh my God, Claudia, I saw everything. You were incredible. I want to hire you for the three-day prison riot scene at the state pen." All I could do was laugh to keep from crying. And give up moviemaking. Forever.

Friends and family members were horrified by my movie tale. Almost all of them asked why we would continue to live in such a place. It got me to thinking about it and I realized it had to do with the culture in the area. I came to realize that our neighbors had learned to "normalize" sensational events and because Thomas and I had lived among them for so many years we simply absorbed the coping mechanism.

It worked something like this: A traumatic event occurred and we all became traumatized for a while. We dealt with it in different ways, but all of us seemed to come out of in about the same way. We knew that life goes on and there would undoubtedly be more drama ahead. The events were simply normalized rather than sensationalized. It made it easier to move on through life, and we tried to learn something from it. And we all knew that it wouldn't be long before we could start laughing at the absurdity of it all.

Charlie Harrington told me he wanted to hire me, to work with him on other films, but he couldn't imagine my wanting to leave our quiet life in San Ignacio. We had a good laugh over that, but he was right. There never was another film shot in the village. Location scouting crews came occasionally, but things had changed. For one thing, the dirt road into the village and around the plaza had been paved. And one by one, the Drinkers began to pass away. It turned out that, in the eyes of the filmmakers, both of those features had been part of the charm of the place and two of the main reasons they had chosen San Ignacio.

The Drinker security guards had performed beyond everyone's expectations. They had extinguished two small fires on different occasions in the middle of the night: one of them at Macario's place, the other in a shed on the back road. The Columbia security manager was impressed by the team's professionalism, and we in the village were proud of the men for honoring their roles.

As I handed each man his check, some of us had tears in our eyes. They thanked me again and again, for having faith in them and for the great movie experience. Every single one of the Drinkers assured me that he had had a great time being a security guard. Each man had earned around three thousand dollars. In their world, that was a lot of money. As soon as the last film trucks rolled out of the village, the Drinkers began a celebration party that went on for over two months.

Comanche had finally made peace with the construction crew. He was the first person on the scene every morning as the sets were being dismantled. It took nearly three days to get things cleared out. Movie companies were usually generous about giving community members building materials that they would not be using again. Comanche wound up with just about everything left behind. The man was much too shy to sign on as an extra, but he did seem to get into the spirit of moviemaking.

Accidental Anthropologists

Billy Bob Thornton asked me to tell my neighbors that it had been an honor for him and the crew to be a part of our little village community during the shoot. We were all invited to the premier that would be shown in Santa Fe a few months later, but Thomas and I were the only ones to attend. I had gone door to door with the invitation, but our neighbors had no interest whatsoever in seeing the final result. All the moviemaking excitement had been quite enough for the entire village. It was a wrap!

29

Epilogue for Roque Romero

A most amazing thing happened to me after "All the Pretty Horses." Any time Roque Romero saw me walking to the post office, he would go out of his way to greet me. Every time, the man would bow slightly in front of me and reach out to shake my hand.

He always said, "Hello, Mrs. Clavel. How are you today?" That went on for years after the movie. One time, he approached me at La Tienda to ask whether I might have two dollars for gas. I said, "Roque, all I have is a five-dollar bill, but you'll need it all or you'll never make it home." He was riding with someone, and people usually charged for giving a ride to the store. Roque promised to pay me back when his Social Security check came. Thomas and I had never given money to anyone believing that it would be repaid.

One day a few weeks later, I was in the post office when Roque walked in. He approached me, put a five-dollar bill in my hand, thanked me again for the loan, and left. Perfecto was standing behind the counter with his mouth open. It took him a while to blurt out, "I can't believe what I just saw. That man has never, I mean never, ever, paid back anybody money he borrowed."

Claudia Clavel

I thought back to the movie shoot, when I had confronted Roque about his bullying and he turned into a little boy in front of my eyes. I told Perfecto that I thought Roque saw me as a mother figure, and when I dared confront him, like most bullies, he caved.

A few months later, Roque was waiting for me when I stepped out the post office door. He said, "Mrs. Clavel, do you have time to talk?" I assured him I did have time, and he went on, "I'm just coming from the doctor, and he told me I have lung cancer. He said I probably have just a short time to live, and I wanted to tell you." We stood facing one another for a moment, both of us with tears in our eyes. The next thing I knew, the two of us were holding onto one another, crying.

Roque was gone a couple months later, and while I was relieved the man no longer had to suffer, I felt his loss. However, when I heard the funeral bell ring, it took me a moment to realize it was for Roque's burial Mass. A huge feeling of conflict came over me as I ran out to look toward the church to see if people were arriving.

I was surprised to see that friends and relatives had already gathered beneath the big cross in front of the church. That meant the church was full. The mourners would remain standing there, praying throughout the Mass, because that was the tradition in the valley. Funerals had always been right up at the top of special village events. On the one hand, I wanted to honor that, but on the other hand, I had hardly known Roque. However, everybody in the valley knew about the movie escapades, so it came as no surprise to me that I would feel conspicuous in that group of mourners. I chose not to go to Roque's funeral.

A couple of hours after the funeral Mass and the dinner at the community center, a car drove up our driveway

Accidental Anthropologists

and honked. It was Perfecto and Pilar coming from the gathering. Perfecto rolled down his window, and after formal greetings, said to me, "Where were you? Why didn't we see you in church?" I was aghast at his tone of voice and said, "I barely knew Roque. And our relationship hadn't been exactly cozy, at least up until the very end."

Perfecto's voice softened as he went on about the funeral. He said, "We are a family here in San Ignacio, and you and Thomas are part of that family, the same as Roque. We each have to honor those who have been taken from us, because they are one of God's children, and part of our family."

30

Sixto, aka Comanche

Some time after "All the Pretty Horses" rode out of town, one late spring morning, Sixto rang my doorbell. When I opened the door, he thrust his right arm forward from behind his back to reveal a bouquet of lilacs in his outstretched hand. That simple act would have floored any of our village neighbors, had they happened upon the scene. However, that was highly unlikely since we were up on top of the hill, off the beaten path. Over a number of years, Sixto would create a worn pathway from his place down below to our house. The sole purpose of the path was getting him to his job as our creative builder during the warm months. Thomas and I saved as much money as possible during winter and then built until the money ran out. We were somewhat relieved when that happened, for then we were left alone to create, willy-nilly, jumping from one creative project to another. Such a silly term, but it described us perfectly.

It was also one of the reasons we so admired Sixto as a builder, for he operated pretty much on the same wavelength. He thought nothing about my running out in the middle of a project to tell him I had changed my mind about building an interior wall or two. In fact, he would probably agree with me that the change was a good idea.

Claudia Clavel

We often shared a laugh about what a contractor would say to me under the same circumstances.

Sixto had not always been so accommodating. In fact, there were times during our early years when he was downright terrifying. The man had a reputation as a thief and troublemaker, the most despised man in the village. More than one person pointed out to me that Thomas and I might have been the only people in the village who would even talk to him. We always referred to him as Mean Sixto, but among villagers, he was known as Comanche. His reputation went back so far, people had probably forgotten how it ever started. It didn't take long for me to figure out that Sixto was one angry guy. He resented anybody who had more than he did.

Since virtually everyone in the village was related by blood, property sometimes created schisms within families. Traditionally, sons were the recipients of inherited property, unless they had become the "black sheep" of the family. In that case, they often found themselves left out completely. Most of the feuds were based on who inherited what property, and the feuds often spilled over in a myriad of ways; but never in regards to a marriage celebration or funeral of a relative or old schoolmate. On those occasions, all bad feelings were put aside for the duration of the event.

One hot, dusty morning, I went down to Sixto's place to retrieve an apron that had been on my clothesline. One of his dogs had pulled it off the line. I saw Brownie running down the hill with my apron in his mouth, part of it dragging on the ground. It was my first time on Sixto's turf, and there were four guys standing in a group, smoking. I approached, laughing, as I told him about his thief dog and my apron. Without a word, Sixto quickly disappeared around a corner of his house. He returned

Accidental Anthropologists

with a big grin on his face, holding the swiped apron. As he handed it to me, one of the guys said, "Wow, Comanche, even your dog's a thief." My neighbor didn't seem to take offense, and we all had a good laugh.

Over time, I learned that Sixto hadn't been born in San Ignacio, but his mother and maternal grandparents were natives of the village. His father had been born in San Juan Pueblo, and Sixto had inherited his father's Pueblo native features. He lived with his parents in Española until he was thirteen years old. It was then the boy tied a long wire around his dog's neck and wrapped the other end around his young waist. The two of them walked to San Ignacio to reach his grandparents' home. The 70-mile journey took several days. The boy felt he could no longer take the beatings from his father, and, without a word, his grandparents took him in, and he never returned to live with his parents. A simple act sealed Sixto's fate. To village people, because of his father's heritage and the fact that Sixto had not been born in San Ignacio, he would forever be considered an outsider. From then on, the boy was always on the fringe of any gathering that took place.

Seasons in the valley unfolded organically. The first hint of warm air automatically set certain habits into motion: chairs began to appear on front *portal*. They were lined up in rows and filled with bodies of various ages, shapes and sizes, depending on family makeup. After supper, which was always at five o'clock no matter what the season, everyone moved out to the *portal*.

Summer evenings were times for socializing. What often started as a family gathering might turn into a little fiesta, as neighbors wandered in and out of yards. Usually, the men would form a group, standing off to the side of the *portal*, leaving the women to gather in the

Claudia Clavel

chairs. The women's talk simply ran up and down the row, and no one ever felt left out. Or moved a chair.

Neighbors told me that Sixto would often show up during the evening gatherings, but he never joined the core group. The man was never seen in the sun without sunglasses, and that alone upset folks. They couldn't tell who he was looking at. The outcast would stand off to the side, leaning up against a truck or wall. Then he would pull out a knife and began to whittle on some little piece of wood.

Sixto never joined in conversations. He just stood with shaded eyes, flicking the long knife against the wood. The longer the whittler kept it up, the more agitated the male group became, until at some point of collective consciousness, the group jumped the outcast and beat the crap out of him. I was told that being beaten up never deterred Sixto, and he continued the pattern for years.

Eventually, Sixto realized he should change his behavior. Part of it had to do with age and a very deep need to be part of the community. He talked to me about that, and I was moved by his awareness that he wanted to change in order to make it happen. Sixto stopped trying to take advantage of people and situations. He became more generous, and actually offered assistance without being asked. Over the years, the transformation was remarkable, and because of that, we began to hire him to help us work on our building projects.

In summer, I took lunch out to whoever might be working with us. During cold months, they were invited in to sit at our table. It was during that time that Sixto and I really got to know one another. As a result, a memorable event occurred: everyday I read Newsweek during lunch, and on that day, the morning newspaper was lying near-by. Sixto and I sat down to eat, and my guest asked if I would read the headlines to him. He wasn't shy about telling me that he didn't know how to read. He said he could write simple words and numbers but could not string words into a sentence. That is when I began to read the newspaper, or a Newsweek article to Sixto every day we ate lunch together.

One summer, Pelita Daniel and Brave Eagle moved into San Ignacio. While the movers were hauling furniture into the house, Sixto walked across the Plaza to confront Pelita. Without a hello, he said, "I'm Comanche. You don't look like you belong here. You need to put that furniture back in the truck and move on."

Of course, he meant to be intimidating, but he had met his match in Pelita, who was Navajo. She fired back, "I can tell I'm more Indian than you, and you'd better back off." Defeated, the bully sort of huffed, as he turned and headed home. They eventually worked out a truce, especially after Sixto learned about Pelita's husband; Brave Eagle was considered by many to be the biggest, badass Indian in the USA. That made a big impression on the bully. And it didn't take long for Pelita to work her spell on the troublemaker. Not only was she a beauty; she was a diplomat as well.

From then on, Sixto became Comanche to Pelita and remained Sixto to me. It was another instance of people in the area introducing themselves either by their given name or a nickname. Only they knew why they chose it or gave it to a particular person.

It took a long time before Thomas and I became aware of how people used names. Some of the first people we met introduced themselves using their nicknames. Others were more formal and used their given names. We never thought much about it until a few years later. Chato was a perfect example. At first, through Perfecto, we knew him as Filadelfio. However, through our neighbor, who was his aunt, we knew him as Chato. Interestingly, Filadelfio later introduced himself to us as Chato. That probably had something to do with the outcome of his trial, when Thomas had been jury foreman.

I also noticed that if someone dropped by our house while Chato was working, before I could introduce him, he would rise from his tile-setting job, stick out his hand and introduce himself as Filadelfio. I noticed other neighbors doing much the same. It was a matter of using a more familiar name with someone you had a friendly relationship with. Sort of like the use of *tú* versus *usted* in Spanish to denote the level of a relationship. The use of a formal name indicated you did not know the person well or it was a business transaction. Thirty years later, we had many double-named friends, and we understood how it worked. And I needn't have worried. They always took care of the introductions themselves.

Comanche began doing work for Pelita and Brave Eagle, and they always invited him in for a meal and conversation. Because of that simple act, the man's knowledge base continued to grow. Comanche became more interested in news and soon became a nightly news junkie, watching every program he could find.

One summer afternoon, Pelita and I were having lunch on her front patio. Comanche was off to the side, working on a stucco job. He stopped for a moment and leaned up against a wall, with one leg bent, listening as we women sat talking about world affairs. In a flash, he pushed himself toward us, nearly shouting, "Well, according to the BBC, this is what's going on." Pelita and I howled with laughter, as I said, "Wow, Sixto, now you have become a global news junkie." We all beamed with pride. By that time, Sixto/Comanche had become a friend

Accidental Anthropologists

and indispensable handyman to us both. Although, he still remained an outsider in the village social scene.

In spite of Sixto's reputation and jealous streak, the man had the most positive attitude about life on a daily basis. He also had a keen sense of humor, like most of his neighbors. Humor in the culture sprang out of everyday happenings: some trivial occurrence that could be turned into a joke, simply due to a different viewpoint. Sometimes, black humor surfaced around something really awful. However, laughter in any form helped soften the sharp edges of tragedies that happened all too often. Over the years, we came to treasure the ironic sense of humor among our neighbors, for it fit with our own as a coping skill. Amongst us all, being able to laugh at one's self seemed to keep the continuity flowing in the valley. Humor that transcended poverty, addictions, sadness and abuses, self-imposed and otherwise. It helped to keep us all going. Laughter seemed to carry people to heaven.

When he was younger, Sixto had worked in Albuquerque as a bridge construction ironworker, so he had absolutely no fear of heights. He was also the only man we had ever seen who could bend with straight knees and place his flattened hands on the floor. That is the way he laid a brick floor or nailed down a deck. I once marveled as I watched Sixto create a scaffold out of small logs for a job he was doing plastering a wall. Every time he had to make the scaffold higher, he would swing up like a monkey and jump up and down on the boardwalk to make it secure enough to walk on with a bucket of cement. I asked him where he learned to create such a functional scaffold and laughed at his reply, "I was watching a program on PBS about the pyramid builders and got the idea from them."

Claudia Clavel

A big surprise came when I first heard Sixto singing while he worked. He was one of the few workers who didn't bring a radio with him on the job, or crank up the one in his vehicle. He had a very good voice and sang all the Old Spanish songs. It was a treat for me in summer when that music drifted in through my kitchen screen door. Any time that I took something out to him, he had a little story to tell about his life in the village as a child or some remembrance of a bunch of guys down on the plaza, playing guitars and singing into the darkness. He said it was not uncommon for neighbors to bring supper to the musicians, for the people considered music a gift.

There was a time when Sixto spent several days re-roofing Thomas' old shop. The guy was so in tune with everything around him, he began to notice barking dogs out by the cemetery. He spent the morning working and never sang, because he was listening intently to the sounds. Just before lunch, Sixto hollered for me to come out of the house. From the top of the roof, the man grew very serious as he explained to me what he was hearing. He could tell by individual barks that a pack of dogs had formed, and they were obviously after a kill. It was calving time, so that would be the object of their attention.

Dogs forming packs were a problem. Thomas and I once witnessed an event during one of our walks out by the railroad tracks. That time, it was a foal, and it was surrounded by a pack of dogs. One of the dogs in the middle of the circle kept nipping at the foal's legs in order to take it down. Thomas ran for the owner, and they returned with a gun. The dogs instinctively knew their fate and slunk away, saving the young horse from a terrible death.

Sixto told me to run in and phone Altagracia, who lived off the plaza. Her brother, Sabino, had a small herd of cattle exactly where the barking was coming from.

Accidental Anthropologists

Altagracia told me they had been losing calves to coyotes or dogs, and she quickly called her brother. They were grateful to Sixto for his keen observations. For years, I continued to learn more of that art from the man who noticed everything.

We eventually finished our major building projects, and, after Thomas retired, we stopped hiring people to help us. Every now and then, Sixto would show up in front of our porch. He rarely knocked, but would sing out, "Claudia or Thomas, where are you?" He usually brought us a little seedling or some leftover building supplies that he thought Thomas might be able to use. We were always happy to see our neighbor and share a few laughs over something trivial. Moreover, we were sure of a story or two.

Sixto's dogs usually joined Thomas as he passed their gate on his walk to the post office. With wagging tails, Brownie and Blackie jumped around with joy as they walked with him all the way home, right to the door. Thomas said that was because he always placed meat scraps on a big, flat rock down at the end of our driveway. The dogs anticipated the treat the minute Thomas walked out the door. He named that spot: Lucky Dog Rock.

31

Weekly Bread Distribution

It was early in April when my friend Ramona Ramon phoned to ask whether I would like to be part of a free bread distribution group that met every Friday at La Tienda. A woman named Gloria who lived in an area closer to Santa Fe had organized the project. She had friends who owned a high-end bakery/café in the city and who shared her interest in animal rights. Because of that connection, the business donated all their leftover bread from the café and local markets. At the end of each week, Gloria picked up whatever they had and drove it to the valley volunteers for distribution to poor folks.

Our neighbors were delighted to receive the bread gratis. The volunteers' role was not only to deliver the bread but also to tell the recipients about a Santa Fe organization that offered free spaying and neutering of cats and dogs. There were four of us distributors, and I was the only one who didn't have a pet.

Up until the free clinics, animals in the valley had never enjoyed the same service as those in the city. No one thought of birth control for a cat or dog. Between owls and coyotes, domestic animals usually had short lives. Some considered that a form of animal birth control.

Claudia Clavel

Not long after the bread distribution began, the mobile clinic paid a visit to the valley. It was quite a sight when the huge SPCA surgical unit arrived from Santa Fe, offering free service to pet owners. The volunteer vets and technicians spayed or neutered sixty-three animals over a two-day period. By the second day, people were being turned away, so the turnout was impressive. I made soup for the volunteers.

Local interest in the clinic grew from there. Over time, we distributors thought that perhaps the bread had played a part in raising awareness about spaying and neutering. Gloria's only role was to pick up the bread and deliver it to the volunteers. It was up to us to divide the load and distribute to as many people as possible in each of our villages and surrounding areas.

Sometimes, there was a huge amount of bread, and other times, not so much. We had to divide it out accordingly. We never knew what the delivery might contain: from whole wheat bread to spelt to native sourdough. Just when our neighbors got used to one kind, there would be a huge shift, with nothing but long baguettes or big round sheepherders loaves. Every once in a while, there was everyone's favorite: raisin bread. We became adept at getting people to try something new, not an easy task in those days. However, after a while, we adopted a casual attitude of take it or leave it.

I think we all enjoyed the opportunity to stop for a bit and visit with our neighbors, and we received much gratitude for our efforts. It took a while, but then villagers became excited by the random selections, sometimes shouting out, "What about that big round loaf?" or "I'm beginning to like the one full of seeds." I never grew tired of Friday bread deliveries because they had become a big social event in my life. It also introduced me to Agustina,

Accidental Anthropologists

one of the bread distributors, who lived outside San Ignacio. The woman was such an animal lover, we swore that she scooped up road kill and took it home to nurse it back to life.

Agustina was an animal rescue volunteer. Sometimes, she had up to forty cats and dogs that she tended to with great devotion and affection. I was amused during a cold snap to learn that the woman fashioned outfits for all her animals. She used clothing she found at thrift shops, namely sweaters and sweatshirts. Agustina would cut up an old sweater, creating four leg openings around the front button area, and then fasten the sweater on the underbelly of the animal, providing warmth during freezing weather. She tried to coordinate colors, with pink for the females and blue for the males. However, the color range often varied, creating a patchwork effect. Except for one small bulldog that she dressed in a black sweatshirt with a turtleneck. As Carmelita, one of the distributors, said, "That dog looked like a little macho biker."

That is when I had to drive over to see for myself. Sure enough, there were all those scraggly animals dressed to the hilt, parading around Agustina's yard. We both started laughing, but Agustina's laughter came from the joy she took in creating the outfits. The animal lover was as poor as a church mouse, but I never heard her complain. I liked her and admired her dedication and creativity. Agustina, like most people in the area, had a great sense of humor, which surely helped in her constant state of poverty. She usually drove up on free-bread Fridays in a beat-up old station wagon with no brakes or reverse gear. As a result, she had to park in the middle of La Tienda's parking lot.

Agustina's station wagon was a sight; occasionally there was a lettuce crate on the roof, filled with donated produce she had picked up at some market in town. After a twenty-five-mile trip, wind-whipped lettuce leaves could be seen clinging to the sides of the crate. Her car was filled to the roof with expired-food containers and more produce that she would pass on to those even less fortunate. Once in a while, Agustina arrived from town with a rescued dog or cat crammed amid her donated goods. With all that food on hand, Agustina became a very creative cook for her animals.

One early spring Friday when we met at La Tienda, Agustina was climbing out of her car when I noticed her hair shimmering in the sunlight. I mean really shimmering. The woman was in her mid-fifties, and she had blond hair without a trace of gray. She always had it tied up in a ponytail. When I looked closer, I saw she had tied on a fake blond fall over her own hair with a pink ribbon. The fall was like Barbie doll hair, and it glistened with the sun shining on it. I asked Agustina about it, and she said she had just come through a big dental procedure that had her face swollen out of proportion. The swelling had finally gone down, and she was so happy that day, the fall was to celebrate the occasion.

None of us knew anyone quite like Agustina. I had heard about her before the bread group from someone who used to take dog and cat food to her when she lived in her car. That was before she and Modesto, her husband, found the funkiest old trailer to move onto their seven sacred acres. Modesto had finally found a job, but he had to work out of town, so Agustina was left on her own to take care of all those animals.

The woman was always upbeat, grateful and happy. Love seemed to surround her, and whenever we met at La Tienda, Agustina threw herself into my arms, shouting, "I love you, I love you." She never gave up on

Accidental Anthropologists

faith or hope in her passion for rescuing animals, and her intense faith paid off. Eventually, she started being paid for her efforts through animal activist groups. It was enough to provide a modest living for her and Modesto and their beloved animals. In addition, there was a bonus for the couple: a donated van for transporting rescued animals.

One season turned into another as the group returned on Fridays and waited for Gloria to show up with the weekly bread. The four of us leaned against our cars and talked until the bread van arrived. We heard bits and pieces of each other's lives, but there was never time for in-depth conversation because the minute the bread arrived, we were busy dividing it and loading our cars. With no preservatives, that leftover bread had a short shelf life, so we were off.

A few months later, by the end of fall, something came over Gloria that none of us could figure out. The bread connection began to unravel, like one of Agustina's old dog sweaters, caught on a barbed-wire fence. There seemed no way to stop the progression, but by then, we all agreed: For a few months, a lot more than bread got passed around the valley.

32

Enchiladas and the Cemetery Meeting
Or
Traditional Democracy in Action

Thomas and I received a phone call from the secretary of
the San Ignacio Community Center board telling us of a
meeting that would be held that Sunday evening at the
center regarding the cemetery. Euservia Valdez explained
that at a recent meeting at the mother church in San
Xavier del Vado, an intriguing question had been raised
that required the people of San Ignacio to gather and
debate the issue of just who had burial rights.

Long ago, the Catholic Archdiocese had designated
the seven village churches in the valley as "missions." The
mother church had jurisdiction over the missions. The
parish priest drove to each village once a month to conduct Mass. In times past, a parish priest might have spent
years in the same church and community. However, after
the mission designation, priests were assigned to the
valley for no more than two years each. In addition, they
were given the title "mission priest." The short assign-
ments were never easy for the parishioners, because there
wasn't enough time to establish tight bonds with their
spiritual leader. During our time in the valley, we watched

Claudia Clavel

a series of dedicated men move in and out of the parish house.

Not all priests were well received, but the all-time favorite had to be Father Tre, a Vietnamese priest with a heavy accent. Not being Catholic, we attended Mass infrequently: village religious events, funerals and an occasional wedding. As a result, we didn't keep up with the priest of the moment, so we were sometimes surprised in church to hear a new foreign accent. An East Indian, for example, or an Irish priest just arrived from Ireland. Our neighbors were open and welcoming to foreign priests, but they had a hard time when someone new wanted to change things in their religious world.

A new Italian priest, Father Vicente, started off with a creative flair that had me hitting the brakes as I drove past the church. The man brought with him large clay planters filled with brilliant red geraniums that he lined up across the dazzling-white plastered wall in front of the church. It was a stunning sight, but it did not endear him to the congregation, for there were strings attached to the beauty. The priest began to admonish his parishioners for not dressing up on Sundays. He told them he would prefer to have the women forgo tee shirts and jeans. He asked people to wear dress shirts and dresses and attend Mass as though it was a special event.

Father Vicente put everyone to work, and a lot was accomplished during his time. He had men plant double rows of large piñon trees along the walk in front of the church. With his red geraniums aglow behind the new trees, the church had never looked more beautiful. The poor Father could not stop lecturing his flock, though, and it was not long before he was reassigned to Albuquerque. Sadly, he took the red geraniums with him. However, the piñon trees continued to thrive, so it wasn't a total loss.

Accidental Anthropologists

It was an American priest, however, who came up with the idea of the mother church taking over control of the San Ignacio cemetery. Coincidentally, someone from the village happened to be at the church meeting when the proposal was made. Most of the mission villages had been running out of cemetery space for some time. Each village had a land grant that allotted so many acres, and San Ignacio wound up having more land than the other villages. Because of that fact, the priest had decided that all burials in the valley should take place in the San Ignacio cemetery.

The village cemetery had expanded twice over time, and during our time, it grew again. A new fence had recently gone up around the new area, which doubled the size of the burial site. There was room for more expansion, but that wasn't the point. It was a territorial issue, and histories among the valley villages. It had to do with community, and who should be allowed a place in the hallowed ground. The meeting was held to decide whether people outside the village had the right to be buried in the San Ignacio cemetery.

The cemetery meeting was one of the largest Thomas and I had ever attended. The community center was packed with parishioners, as well as those who had not attended Mass in years. With the exception of a funeral, baptism or wedding, we pretty much fit into that category. However, I had helped clean and decorate the church during the yearly Posada and the Feast Day of San Ignacio, and I always brought food. Thomas had cleaned the pigeon guano out of the belfry on several occasions. Due to our contributions to the religious community, Thomas and I had been told by a *mayordomo* of the village a long time ago that we could be buried in the cemetery. We took that as a compliment, though we had been talking about cremation as an alternative. Our interest in the meeting was to witness how issues like that were worked out among people in the community.

Our local politician, State Senator Isaac Medina, brought the meeting to order. He held up a piece of paper that he said was the deed to San Ignacio. In the deed, there was a clause that spoke of "successors" to the cemetery. The senator, a lawyer, said the deed would have to be examined by lawyers familiar with land grants. They could determine for the last time who had the right to be buried in the village cemetery. Isaac did say, "The deed makes clear that the San Ignacio cemetery has always been nondenominational and not exclusively set aside for Catholics, practicing or not."

There was much murmuring among the crowd as they tried to digest all the facts. Urbano Valdez, a Community Center board member, stood next and spoke to his neighbors: "Let's use enchiladas as a metaphor in addressing the issue of burial. Suppose you own property in the village and are not Catholic, but you bring enchiladas every year to the Posada and Feast Day dinners. Does that get you into the cemetery?"

That spoke directly to us, for that was what we had always done, even though in our case it was usually salad. Everyone was looking directly at us, and you could see they were thinking hard about the question. One by one, heads began nodding, and then hands went up, as our neighbors voted to allow Thomas and me burial rights.

Urbano went on, "If you were born in San Ignacio but moved away for many years, can you come back to be buried in your homeland?" The crowd readily agreed to that request. Then another question, "If you were born in San Ignacio, but never attended Mass, do you have the right to be buried in the cemetery?" After much thought

Accidental Anthropologists

and discussion, there was agreement: By birth, everyone had that right. A couple of the Drinkers attended, and we could see that they were visibly relieved by the decision.

The senator said he would call another meeting after the land grant lawyers had looked at the deed. However, some important questions had already been answered. Thomas and I thought we had witnessed a very fair and humane democratic process. The priest who thought up the cemetery take-over by the mother church was soon reassigned. Moreover, the reason for another meeting was all but forgotten.

33

Religious, Social and Political Events

Whenever we heard the church bell toll, we could be assured of one of two certainties: Either a Mass was being announced, or someone had died. It wasn't until Pilar asked me to ring the bell that I realized that there were two distinctive techniques for the task. The ring for Mass was decidedly more enthusiastic than the ring announcing someone's passing. For a death, Pilar told me, I should ring the bell slowly and deliberately three times. She emphasized that I ring the bell with reverence.

Because Thomas and I were not Catholic, some in the village voiced concern at the time, about my being asked to ring the bell. Even though I helped clean the church for various events throughout the years, in the eyes of the parishioners that did not entitle me to take part in church affairs. In San Ignacio, that was a religious issue. However, that day, no one else was around, and Pilar wasn't physically able to climb the steep, narrow stairs to the belfry, so she asked me to do it.

My bell ringing initiation happened a long time ago, and I had all but forgotten it until years later when I heard the death knell being rung again. It reminded me of some of the nuances within the culture. There were other rituals, and omens around death that were also foreign to us, and we were surprised over time by how some of those things influenced our lives.

Birds as symbols have long played a part in Native American and Hispanic cultures. A young Hispanic friend who had lost her husband and son in a traffic accident, learned about the bird connection during grief counseling. Precilla was told that a bird would often visit the survivor shortly after the loss of a loved one. Among some groups, it was almost expected. My young friend told me that she did have that experience shortly after her loss. During our years in San Ignacio, I was visited several times by a bird in similar situations. Once it was shortly after the death of Herminio, Precilla's father. We had been close friends with her family for nearly forty years.

Within a week or so after Herminio's passing, I was sitting at the kitchen table with the back door open, when I heard a strange whistling sound. It sounded like a man's whistle, and at first, I thought it was someone coming to call. I went to the door, stepped out and looked around. It took a moment, and then I saw a medium-size, rather drab-looking bird sitting not too far away. The bird whistled again several times. The bird's call was completely foreign to me. I did not move and suddenly felt goose bumps washing over my body. I knew in that instant, it was Herminio, coming to say goodbye. The reason I was sure enough to write about the experience came three years later, as Herminio's wife, Romanita, lay dying.

I had been visiting Romanita every week at her daughter's home in Santa Teresa. My friend was living out the remainder of her days in a lovely suite of rooms that Agnes and David had built for her after she was diagnosed with lymphoma. Toward the end, I remembered the whistling bird and began telling her the story. Romanita looked at me through eyes that had grown wide and then

Accidental Anthropologists

said, "Claudia, Herminio knew that bird. He heard it one day when he was out on his horse, Amigo. When he came home, he told me about it. He said he had never seen the bird before, nor heard that call. Herminio said it sounded like a man's whistle. In fact, he called it the 'man bird.' We both thought it was odd."

Romanita became excited as she went on with her story. "Herminio and I were on the front *portal* a little later when the 'man bird' landed on the corner of the roof. The bird began to whistle, and it did sound like a man, whistling to get your attention. Then it flew away. We never saw it again."

Romanita and I remained silent in thought for a while and then looked at one another with tears in our eyes. The man-bird connection to Herminio had become a real and powerful omen.

When we heard the mournful, three-ring sequence of the church bell, we knew someone had died but not who it was. Even after three decades, we were not part of the phone tree that went into action the moment something out of the ordinary occurred. We were still outsiders in the village, and that is the way we preferred to live. To be a real part of the village family, you had to immerse yourself in it, and that could include all the extended families. Being part of the village family meant you attended all the weddings, baby showers, and graduations, et al. The numbers could be huge. We tried that for a while at the beginning but soon became overwhelmed. Besides, we had our own family and a large group of old friends. Even though they lived far away, we were close and stayed connected throughout the years. Our summer and fall seasons were often filled with houseguests, young and old. Most of the time, Thomas and I stuck to the village rituals, where we could enjoy our neighbors on special occasions. Over time, everyone understood, so it was never an issue.

Every church in the valley had a *mayordomo*, or in the case of a married couple or two different people, *mayordomos*. Because the village mission churches were small, people in the community volunteered to take turns. *Mayordomos* served for one year and were in charge of all church activities, including maintenance. Most often, family members were involved in helping with restoration chores, especially when they were on a large scale. Over the years, I had observed folks coming up with some creative projects for their beloved church. With Pilar, it was always altar cloths. Perfecto's choices were more pragmatic, like cleaning out the belfry when pigeon guano piled up above the choir loft. They eventually sealed the roof, and that put a stop to the problem. Some years, the church was re-plastered on the outer adobe walls, and that would involve the entire village. Other projects were not as ambitious.

Eutimio and Euservia Valdez once surprised the congregation when they painted all the pews a new color and added gold-painted images on the pew sides. But, they went beyond that when they padded all the kneelers. You could almost hear the sighs of relief as elders knelt to pray.

Eutimio and Thomas had always shared a creative building passion, especially when it came to using whatever was lying around. It shouldn't have been too surprising when Eutimio turned up with his greatest cast-off score. He and Euservia had been playing bingo at a Jesuit school in Santa Fe for over twenty-five years when they were told the school had been sold. All the religious artifacts had to be removed.

Accidental Anthropologists

Someone at the school who knew the couple asked Eutimio if he would like to buy a marble statue of San Ignacio-for two thousand dollars. What the man neglected to say was the fact that San Ignacio's head had been broken off during moving. And, he added, "Oh yeah, there are two smaller marble angels that go with the statue, but their wings are broken a bit."

Eutimio went to look at the statues and started to laugh as he said, "The statue has no head. You have angels with broken wings. We are a poor village. Why don't you just give them to us?"

"But these are marble, and worth a lot of money. We have to sell them," responded the man. Eutimio just shook his head and headed home.

About a week later, a truck pulled up to the front of the church, and the statues were unloaded. San Ignacio's head was in a box, carefully wrapped in bubble wrap. The deliveryman told Eutimio the village church could have the statues after all, for no one would buy them in their damaged state. Eutimio knew of a local sculptor who worked in marble, and the artist said he could put San Ignacio's head back on but couldn't repair the angels' wings.

That didn't bother Eutimio, for he knew that none of it mattered to all of us who lived here. We all knew, that a reconnected head and broken wings didn't always tell the whole story. The statues were a lovely addition to the village churchyard.

The village of San Ignacio, like all the other villages in the valley, celebrated two major religious events a year: the *Funcion*, as it was called, held in March to celebrate the Feast Day of San Ignacio, and the Posada, which took place just before Christmas. In addition, every year, to celebrate the feast day of San Xavier, the patron saint of the mother church, there was a fiesta in the village of the same name. Everyone in the valley was invited to the Fiesta de San Xavier, for it was a celebration of gathering as a community.

The fiesta was celebrated with a parade, carnival games, and a communal meal. It was also a fundraiser for the church, with each village contributing to the event by sponsoring a game or food booth. Villages took turns being responsible for the midday meal. A big raffle was held, with the top prize usually five hundred dollars. Other prizes might include a side of beef, restaurant meals and cords of wood. One year, we won a cord of wood that came in handy through a cold winter.

One year when Diego, Gabriel and Eloy were in their early teens, Thomas talked them into building a scale model of our village church for the San Ignacio float. The model measured about three feet high by two feet wide and three feet long. The group arrived in the late afternoons to work on the project in the shade of our courtyard. None of the boys attended church, but Thomas convinced them they needed to be part of the parade during the fiesta. It didn't take long before the three of them got into the project with gusto. Church walls were painted white, and the double doors and window frames, brown. They were excited to get the tin roof on, so the belfry could be installed. Thomas found a small brass bell that he hung inside.

The afternoon before the fiesta, all the children in the village gathered at Perfecto and Pilar's house to work on the float. I was in charge of crepe paper and getting everyone organized to stuff little squares of paper into the chicken wire Perfecto had attached to the sides of his long flatbed trailer. We worked until it was too dark to see and were proud of our efforts.

Accidental Anthropologists

That night, the men of the village gathered in the senator's barn while a group of women were clustered around his wife's big restaurant stove in their spacious kitchen.

It was San Ignacio's year to host the fiesta dinner, and each woman had been assigned a dish to serve three hundred people. Amanda, the senator's wife, had pots and pans to accommodate the huge quantities. Her family was donating all the ingredients, so all we women had to do was prepare the recipes. I was assigned Spanish rice and began chopping onions. Pilar saw what I was doing and came over to me, saying, "Claudia, we don't eat onions in our Spanish rice." I looked at her in disbelief and thought about it a moment. Finally, I said, "Pilar, I'm sorry, but you have to let me prepare this dish the way I would do it at home for company." Shaking her head as she turned away, she said, "Nobody will eat it." I told her to leave it to me.

It was great fun; cooking and gossiping with all the women while the men were discussing politics and church functions in the barn. Thomas had hauled the church model to the barn a little earlier, with Diego, Eloy and Gabriel in tow. Because the boys were from different villages and considered "trouble" by some, Thomas wanted them to present their gift to the village men personally. He told the group that the boys had been the principal builders and how much they enjoyed the process. The three teenagers went from man to man, shaking hands and receiving thanks from their elders.

Early on the morning of the fiesta parade, our float was lined up behind the others. Each float had a religious theme. On the San Ignacio float, children sat in front of the little church, tossing out wrapped candies to the crowd lining the road. Every time the float moved, the little bell rang out for all to hear.

Claudia Clavel

It was a bit late when Thomas and I got to the parish hall for dinner, and we hoped there was still food available. Pilar rushed up to us and said, "Claudia, you won't believe it, but everybody liked your Spanish rice. We ran out, because people came back for more. I guess we'll have to add onions from now on."

A political rally was another favorite valley event. Having a politician living in the village was a plus, especially when an election was coming up. We could always be assured of at least a couple of bands and plenty of great food to accompany an afternoon of political candidates, who would be pitching themselves as the best possible vote.

One early September morning, the plaza began filling up with everything needed for a big party. A huge circus-type tent was set up in the middle of the plaza, and it was surrounded on three sides by food preparation equipment. A makeshift stage was put together on the fourth side.

That particular rally was in support of the Democratic gubernatorial candidate, a woman who was running against the first Latino woman to run as a Republican for governor in the state's history. It was to be a very big party. The senator's wife called all the San Ignacio women, asking them to fill their portable roaster ovens with either red or green chile. The political action committee was providing the ingredients. I had to laugh as each of us women hauled our chile down to the food area and found there were six of us, all with brand-new roaster ovens. We declared ourselves "the village roaster brigade," available for any worthy event.

Staring in wonder, we all watched as a man driving a pickup filled with wood, backed a huge, flat, steel cook-top into position. Once he had the giant griddle settled in its spot, the man began unloading and stacking all the wood beneath the stove. He started with kindling and some crumpled newspapers and worked his way to good-size logs. In no time, there was a roaring fire to heat that baby up.

We, the "roaster brigade" ladies: Apolina, Pilar, Rosina, Euservia, Delfinia and I lined up, ready to dish up our signature chiles, (which were more like gravy or soup served in paper bowls.) However, that wouldn't happen until the tortillas were rolled out, and those were being made as we watched. Once a tortilla was made, it was tossed onto the hot griddle to brown slightly. Directly across the hot steel span, fresh green chiles were being laid on the grill to char. Between the aromas of browning tortillas and roasting chile, you could feel the collective swoon among the gathering crowd.

Women from other villages were at the grill. You could see they had experience with the process. Their hands were flying as they peeled hot chiles or rolled out perfect tortilla discs. Inside the community center, more food was being set out, and as the crowd swelled to nearly five hundred, food continued to appear as though by magic.

A succession of three bands entertained us from the stage before the speeches began in late afternoon. We all milled around, visiting with neighbors and perhaps picking up another green chile wrapped in a tortilla hot off the grill. Thomas and I had never enjoyed a political rally as much as we did that one.

During election years when the senator won his race, he threw a village party that went on all night. We didn't attend the festivities, but did enjoy the massive fireworks displays that went on in the plaza below us.

Claudia Clavel

Local people spared no expense when it came to fireworks. One particularly wet summer, we had a Fourth of July party in our summerhouse and were delighted to witness one of the biggest firework displays in memory. The senator decided to surprise, and treat his neighbors to a two-hour extravaganza.

There were about twelve of us in the summerhouse, and we simply hauled our chairs out to the yard and settled in for the show. In earlier days, the monsoon usually began right around the Fourth of July. We always worried that it might rain on the fireworks. Year after year, it began to rain every day the week before the Fourth, but usually, the rain stopped on that special day, so fireworks were guaranteed.

A long time ago, the seven village churches in the valley had been designated as missions. Each village had its own patron saint and annual Feast Day, or *Funcion*. The parish priest, who lived in the San Xavier parish house, rotated among the seven villages to conduct Mass. In San Ignacio, the Mass always took place on the first Saturday evening of the month. Village women spent Friday afternoons cleaning the church and preparing for the next day's Mass. The final touch was the arrangement of several bouquets of fresh flowers on the altar. The choice of flowers was always appropriate to the season. I thought that was particularly creative of the *mayordomo*.

For a number of years, I joined the village women to clean and decorate the church for the Posada Mass at Christmas. When Pilar and Perfecto were *mayordomos*, I helped Pilar cut new altar cloths. She then took them to a woman who loved embroidering the religious symbols on each cloth. From there, another creative woman volunteered to crochet borders. In the process, the women created a completely new set of altar cloths, keeping the tradition alive.

Accidental Anthropologists

In our early years in the village, people took great pride in preparing for the religious celebrations. On the morning of the Posada event, village men gathered wood in order to assemble the small, neatly stacked piles of piñon wood that were called *luminarios*, or bonfires. The woodpiles were spaced around the church and at the homes of participants in the procession. In the evening, as the church bell called the village to Mass, the wood stacks were set ablaze, lighting up the night sky. It was lovely to walk down the hill toward the illuminated church, breathing in the heavenly piñon wood smoke.

At the end of Mass, the statues of San Ignacio and baby Jesus were carried outdoors by church elders. There, the procession formed, led by a group of musicians. The crowd walked slowly around the church, flames lighting up our faces as the guitarists strummed, and everyone sang the old, traditional Spanish songs. If we were lucky, it would be snowing lightly. If we were really lucky, there would be no wind. A little donkey was brought into the village to be part of the pageant. Joseph, portrayed by a young village boy, led the donkey carrying Mary, who was played by a young village girl, to three different houses in the village.

At each house, the group of musicians sang a song in Spanish, asking the homeowners to give shelter to Joseph and Mary. The people assembled inside the house sang a response, denying them entrance. The group then moved on to the second house, where the same request was made. Again, they were refused entry. Finally, at the third house, the singers inside sang to the entire gathering, inviting them to enter for a potluck supper.

In the early days, the large crowd filled every room of the host's old adobe home. We once sat on a bed in a small bedroom with many of our neighbors. We all had paper plates of food balanced on our laps, laughing and visiting while the musicians continued to entertain us. We loved that closeness, with the warmth and smells of wood smoke and chile wafting throughout the house. Years later, the community center offered more space, but it was never quite the same.

The little donkey was given hay as a reward before being loaded onto a truck heading home. The donkey played its role night after night at each village on the Posada roster. The Posada date for each village was determined by drawing numbers out of a hat a few weeks before the event took place. With seven mission churches in the valley, the Posada was held every night of the week in a different village, leading up to Christmas Eve.

That Posada event took place at the mother church in San Xavier during midnight Mass. The infant Jesus was placed in his manger at the significant hour, drawing the pageant to a close. Villagers celebrated the midnight hour with hot chocolate and *bizcochitos*, the iconic New Mexico holiday cookie that remains a favorite. Dinner was never served at this event.

For our village Posada, the women prepared their signature dishes for the celebration, and there was always enough to feed over a hundred people. From the beginning, my specialty was salad. It was my practice to buy leaf lettuce, but I knew that iceberg was the choice of our neighbors, so for the first couple of events, that is what I prepared. However, since nutrition had always been a factor in my choice of foods, I could not keep from introducing some of those foods to our neighbors. I started using leaf lettuce in my salads, and then I took some delight in adding more and more "foreign objects." There had to be no fewer than five chopped vegetables: red onion, red bell pepper, cucumber, zucchini and cherry tomatoes.

Accidental Anthropologists

When I added capers and feta, I waited for some resistance, but none came. One time when I forgot to add capers, Palemon called out, "Hey, what happened to those little green salty things?" There was a memorable salad dressing with a lot of basil and thyme that people enjoyed, even when I switched to olive oil.

A few years ago, the Posada dinner inspired me to try something different. As always, leaf lettuce, but this one with chopped red onion, chunks of orange, Armenian cucumber and chunky feta cheese. The dressing was pomegranate vinaigrette. A little into the meal, there was a shout from Marcos in the crowd, "Claudia, this is the best one yet!"

(Note: One exceptionally hot October afternoon, I knew my reputation with food was established when I took a salad to a funeral dinner in another village. As I was setting it down in the kitchen, a woman approached me and looked in the big bowl. She stepped back to look at my face and then shook her finger at me knowingly, saying, "I know who you are. You're the salad lady from San Ignacio." I enjoyed that title as much as I enjoyed creating salads for my neighbors.)

On a recent cold, windy December evening, as soon as the church bell began tolling to announce Mass, Thomas and I grabbed the salad ingredients and headed out the door. The San Ignacio Posada was about to begin. Once we settled in our pew, I noticed there were far fewer people than in previous years. We were sitting toward the back and couldn't see faces, so we weren't sure who was there. During the singing response, I realized there were no children or young people taking part. All the voices belonged to their parents and grandparents.

It was then I noticed that there were no altar cloths. That came as a shock, for it would be a first. It all seemed very sad from days past, when the church would be packed with people, their voices raised in singing the Old Spanish hymns.

Another change that year was the addition of an accordion player to the small group of musicians who played every year throughout Mass. They played off to the side of the altar, out of sight of the congregation, so Thomas and I were surprised to see a boy around twelve years old playing the accordion as the procession began. The boy played with such joy, he could not stop smiling, and later, in the community center, he played again, sometimes talking to his friends, but never missing a beat. The young musician was bouncing up and down with his instrument as he looked around the room and kept the music going. His smile was infectious. Nasario told us the youngster had taught himself to play and loved performing with the group. I hoped he wasn't too hungry.

The day before, I had bought two big boxes of mixed leaf lettuce and more vegetable ingredients than usual for my Posada salad. Some years, there might be close to a hundred people staying after Mass for the communal meal. This year it was more like forty or fifty neighbors. In the past, you could count three or four roaster ovens lined up, filled with red or green chile. *Posole* and pinto beans were considered staples. Mashed potatoes had never been left out, and you could always find at least one Crockpot of spaghetti tucked in between the roasters. Dinner rolls occupied a special place on the volunteer menu. My salad bowl was big enough to serve many hungry revelers, but with two boxes, I kicked it up a notch. It turned out to be a good move.

When Thomas and I walked into the community center after Mass, the first thing we noticed was the food table: there was only one. Normally, there would have been two or three tables loaded with food. It was even more alarming when we saw just one roaster oven of *posole*. There was one large pan of enchiladas, one Crockpot with Pilar's green chile and a large pan filled with turkey. There was also a huge pan brimming over with dinner rolls. Standing next to the food table, Euservia, a former *mayordomo*, looked totally stressed, actually on the verge of tears. In all our years, there had never been a shortage of food for the Posada dinner, no matter how many people turned out.

Euservia told me no one had contacted anyone in the village to ask for food donations. She said, "This is a reflection on San Ignacio. It's really embarrassing." My first thought was, "Why would we have to be asked, when year after year we always take the same thing?" However, there was something about protocol in the village that we never understood.

Euservia and I stood next to the big pan of dinner rolls, and because we didn't know what else to do, we started tearing buns in half. My friend looked at me with the saddest eyes and said, "Claudia, how are we going to feed all these people?" I was trying to come up with an answer, but nothing came to mind. I just stood there with half a dinner roll in my hand. Without thinking, I replied, "Well, Euservia, we have to think about Jesus, and how he fed the masses with a few loaves of bread." She perked up at that and said, "You're right, we have to keep the faith." Then we both laughed nervously and continued dividing buns as fast as we could.

As people entered from the procession, I noticed many village families were absent. Most of those coming in were visitors. No wonder there was so little food. But what had kept the villagers away?

People stood around, listening to Nasario and his musicians playing Christmas carols and waiting for the priest to say grace. The priest walked over to the food table, but when he saw the meager offerings, he grabbed a dinner roll, muttered something about being on a diet, and headed out the door. The deacon said grace.

Fortunately, there was a lot of turkey, and the roaster oven was full of *posole*. Gregorita doled out the enchiladas in mini-servings, and people did not have to hold back on my salad or the dinner rolls. The dessert table was full enough, and that made people happy, so our neighbors were smiling as they dropped their empty paper plates in the bin.

As everyone was leaving, a relieved Euservia came over and put her arms around me. She said, "Thank you for reminding me about Jesus and the loaves." However, it did make me wonder about where the traditional celebration in San Ignacio was headed.

34

The Good Samaritan and the Horse Funeral

Very recently, at the end of summer, I received a phone call from Pilar, who wanted to chat. She had not driven much in a while so if I hadn't been down to see her, I would get a call and we would catch up on the news in our lives. Pilar was already chuckling as she launched into a story about Perfecto and his involvement in the death of a neighbor's horse. Pilar had always called her husband the Good Samaritan because he was that kind of guy, rushing off to help a friend or neighbor in need. An Anglo couple had moved next door to them a year or so ago. They brought two horses and two goats with them. As with the other five Anglo folks in San Ignacio, the couple was rather shy and reclusive, and they were hesitant about asking for help.

Pilar told me that Adam had phoned the week before, and asked to speak with Perfecto. Adam's wife was quite ill and they were in the process of moving out of the village, when one of their horses dropped dead in front of Adam. He was at a loss as to what to do, so he called his neighbor to ask for advice. Perfecto owned a backhoe, so he walked over to assess the situation, and then called Palemon to come and help. Perfecto drove his backhoe to the site and the three men managed to get the dead horse into the front bucket. They stopped by Arcenio's, and asked him to accompany them up beyond the cemetery so he could help pick out the burial site.

The Good Samaritan dug a very deep hole and as he worked he couldn't stop thinking about Adam's misfortunes, so he decided to take extra care in creating the gravesite. As he told Pilar, "I wanted to make that grave real pretty for the couple." He was about to begin filling in the hole, but Adam said very quietly, "Hold on...hold on a minute," as he headed to his car. He returned with an object he tossed into the grave and Perfecto said, "Okay, here I go with the dirt."

As Perfecto headed toward the opening, Adam said, "Wait a minute...wait just a minute," and once again went to his car where he took out a sheet and blanket. He spread those over the horse and Perfecto said, "Are we ready?" Adam told him to begin filling in the grave, and the backhoe operator began the task of mounding the earth very carefully.

With the task completed, Perfecto wanted to say something to comfort Adam, but just then, Adam said, "Wait just a moment...hold on," and he headed for his car. He returned with a bottle of something, and began to pour it over the mound. He said it was a solution to repel other animals from digging up the grave. By then, the onlookers were beginning to wonder about the ritual, and just when they thought it must surely be over, Adam slowly and quietly said, "Wait a minute...wait another minute," as he took another bottle out of his car. That one was full of whiskey, and he turned to the men and said, "We have to make a toast to my horse." They passed the bottle around, each taking a swig, and then Adam poured the remainder over the earth mound.

Accidental Anthropologists

The village men assumed the funeral had drawn to a close, but Adam stopped them again. He went to his car one last time and brought back a cross, which he gently placed on the grave.

Perfecto said he couldn't hold back as he asked, "Are we finished?" When Adam nodded an assent, Perfecto went on to add, "If I had known it was going to be such an elaborate funeral I would have called the priest."

As the men shook hands, Adam pressed money into Perfecto's hand, but the Good Samaritan said, "I can't take your money. I wouldn't have missed this for the world. This funeral will go down in the history of San Ignacio."

It's that kind of place!

"Stories in families are colossally important.
Every family has stories:
Some funny, some proud, some embarrassing, some shameful.
Knowing them is proof of belonging to the family."

-Salman Rushdie